Every Grain of Rice

Every Grain of Rice

A Taste of Our Chinese Childhood in America

BY

Ellen Blonder AND
Annabel Low

ILLUSTRATED BY

Ellen Blonder

CLARKSON POTTER/PUBLISHERS
NEW YORK

Published by Clarkson N. Potter, Inc.,
201 East 50th Street, New York, New York 10022.
Member of the Crown Publishing Group.

Random House, Inc. New York, Toronto, London,
Sydney, Auckland
http://www.randomhouse.com/

CLARKSON N. POTTER, POTTER, and colophon are
trademarks of Clarkson N. Potter, Inc.

Printed in China

Design by Marysarah Quinn

Library of Congress Cataloging-in-Publication Data
Blonder, Ellen,
Every grain of rice: a taste of our Chinese childhood
in America / by Ellen Blonder and Annabel Low.—1st ed.
Includes index.
1. Cookery, Chinese   2. Chinese American
families.   I. Low, Annabel.   II. Title.
TX724.5.C5B57   1998
641.5951—dc21   97-26276

ISBN 0-609-60102-4

10 9 8 7 6 5 4 3 2 1

First Edition

To Dennis, Molly, and Joel, with love,
and in memory of my parents
—Annabel

With love and gratitude to my parents,
my husband Nick, and daughter Lisa
—Ellen

ACKNOWLEDGMENTS

Love and thanks to Ellen's mother for leading us by the hand around her kitchen and through Chinatown, and spending many patient hours dictating from fifty years' worth of Chinese recipe notes in order to pass down her wealth of knowledge; and to Ellen's father for adding bits of translation, history, wisdom, and lore.

Thanks to Ellen's husband Nick for his enthusiastic, full-hearted support through endless reading and editing, to Annabel's husband Dennis for his moral support, great taste buds, and good humor during this time, to our children Lisa, Molly, and Joel for patience, perspective, and honest opinions, and to Annabel's sister Esther for her belief in this book and the memories she shared with us.

Deepest gratitude for the moral support of many friends, including Peggy Ackley, Juanita Callejas, Dora Choy, Jacki Fromer, Sylvia Garcia-Lechelt, Robin Goodrow, Rhoda Grossman, Bernadette Gutierrez, Jean Hom, Norma Hoshide, Steve Mack, Heather Preston, Patricia Schwarz, Bill Shelley, Rona Weintraub, Martha Weston, Elaine Mae Woo, and Annabel's friends at PG&E and Clorox. Special thanks to Gerald Nachman for reading and advising, to Rita Abrams for her reading, then gathering friends to hear the stories, too, and to Martin Cruz Smith and Emily Smith for invaluable insights, meals, and advice throughout.

To agents Amy Rennert and Sandra Dijkstra, thanks for the faith and for seeing us through. To editor Pam Krauss and art director Marysarah Quinn for taking a chance on us and working with us with such meticulous, heartening care. And to family members who tasted, criticized, improved, and helped us remember until our waists expanded alarmingly, our sides ached from so much laughter, and our hearts overflowed, love and thanks to Bill and Joan, Dewey, Edmond, Julie, David, Joe, and all their spouses and children.

During the writing of this book, we especially felt the spirit of Annabel's parents. We write this book in their honor and in their memory.

CONTENTS

NOTE: Those readers who are new to Chinese cooking or unfamiliar with some of the ingredients or terms used in the recipes may want to review the information regarding menus, techniques, equipment, and ingredients starting on page 185 before beginning to cook. Phonetic Chinese terms are in our native Lungdu dialect.

INTRODUCTION

"Eat every grain of rice," Mother used to say when I was a child. "Every grain counts."

When Father married Mother in China, he proudly gave her gold and jade jewelry for a wedding gift. Though she seldom wore it, she treasured that jewelry. She wrapped it carefully in fine cloth and looked at it often.

Years later, China was at war. Father was in America, unable to get money through to Mother and my siblings in China. Food was scarce, but Mother vowed the family would survive.

She took out her jewelry, gazed at it one last time, and made her decision: she traded the jewelry for five pounds of rice. Those five pounds of rice kept the family from starving. Every grain counted.

—Annabel

connections

ELLEN

In China, a woman's cooking skill was a source of pride for her entire family. A plain woman gained status if she was a good cook. A pretty woman was sneered at if she was not. People pitied her family, but not her. All girls were warned that they had better pay attention in the kitchen if they ever wanted to find a good husband.

Reputations were made by outstanding deftness with a single dish. We grew up listening to long discussions about who made the lightest *lek doi* (Chinese dough-nuts) or the prettiest *ha gow* (shrimp dumplings). We all knew which relative never kneaded her New Year cake properly. Another wound the string too tightly around her *jeng*—bamboo-leaf-wrapped packets of sweet rice—leaving too little room for the rice to expand while cooking. This one undersalted. That one was lazy when washing her greens.

What a difference a generation makes. For all the time we spent helping in the kitchen while we were growing up, we missed that next step of mastering the recipes on our own; we lost our connection to the old ways of cooking. We can teach our daughters how to deal with corporations, but we couldn't pass down the simplest technique for dealing with a taro root.

Perhaps we had to reach midlife to realize something was amiss. Lately, when the family has gathered for holidays, we've reminisced dreamily of long-forgotten dishes that not one of our generation had made since leaving home.

My parents were surprised and delighted to be asked at last to share their wealth of knowledge about food. We asked so many questions that my mother must have wondered but was too polite to ask, "What have you all been *eating* all these years?" She walked us through many Asian markets and dictated recipe after recipe from piles of yellowed notes, adding tidbits of advice from other relatives.

When we started test-cooking, Annabel and I fumbled through our first batch of *jeng*, scooping raw rice into badly folded bamboo leaves. When we lined up the finished packets before boiling them, they all looked a little lopsided and clumsily wrapped, but we grinned with parental pride anyway. Perhaps it wasn't too late to start cooking up some roots.

China to America

ANNABEL

Father was sixty years old when I was born, and Mother, forty. When I was just beginning my life, Father had already lived a full lifetime and Mother was starting a new life in America.

Father was born in China in 1889. There he heard many stories about "Gold Mountain," the Chinese name for America—how the streets were paved with gold, how easy it was to earn money there, and Father believed the stories.

At the age of twenty he came to America intending to earn money and return to China a wealthy man. A photograph taken of him during that time shows a young man with a proud face. His hair is pulled back into a long braid, a queue, the way Chinese men wore their hair at that time, and he is dressed in traditional Chinese attire.

He discovered that the promises of easy money were not true and learned quickly about discrimination. Not long after his arrival, a taunting mob followed him down a street; their jeering turned to violence and as some people held him down, one man chopped his braid off with a knife. When Father was drafted for World War I and showed up for the examination, the official deemed him unfit for service. When he asked why, the official stated that, due to his race, the government could not be sure that he would be loyal to the United States.

Father believed in hard work. He worked during the day and learned English in the evenings. He went where the work was, moving from San Francisco to Chicago, Los Angeles, and Sacramento. He picked fruit, operated a sewing machine, and worked in clothing and dry goods stores before settling in the restaurant business, which he loved.

When Father was thirty-eight, he decided it was time to marry. He returned to China with some of the money he had saved and set about finding a suitable wife. He had heard about Mother, who was said to be pretty and an ideal marriage prospect. Mother was very different from Father. He was mercurial; she was the most patient person I have ever known. He was flamboyant; she preferred to stay in the background. He was a storyteller; she was a listener. But both were strong of spirit and they loved each other.

They were married in 1928; Mother was eighteen years old at the time. China was a poor country, and Father eventually realized he could not support a family sufficiently if he stayed in China. By the time Father decided to go back to

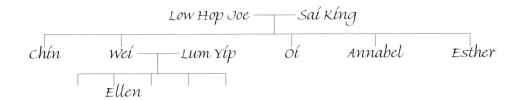

Low Hop Joe —— Sai King

Chin   Wei —— Lum Yip   Oi   Annabel   Esther

Ellen

America, they had a son Chin, a daughter Wei, and Mother was pregnant with a third child Oi. He promised he would soon send for them. They did not know it would be almost sixteen years before they would see one another again, nor did they foresee the hardships ahead.

While Father was in America, Mother lived with her mother-in-law and endured difficult times. Japan invaded China and the Communists were gaining strength. Starvation was widespread and bandits ruled the countryside. Father sent money, but unknown to him, it never reached Mother. Often there was little food on the table, and during the worst times, they dug for roots and worms for food and gathered twigs for cooking and warmth.

Meanwhile, Father continued to make his way in America. The young man in naive Chinese attire who suffered having his braid chopped off had become a confident man of the world who favored the latest fashions. He was mobile and loved the glamour of cities like Chicago and Los Angeles. He discovered his talent for cooking and put his skills to work. At one point he had a restaurant in Los Angeles that was frequented by movie stars. He worked hard all those years and saved his money. He thought of his wife and children constantly, yearning to bring them over.

Because U.S. exclusionary laws prohibited Chinese men from bringing their wives or families to America, Father did not know when he could send for his family. When word came that the exclusionary laws would soon be repealed, Father looked for a home for his family. He heard that

Sacramento was a good place to have a business and rear a family, so he moved there. He and a friend started Hong Kong Cafe, where he worked by day and lived by night so he could save for a house. He was practical in his housekeeping, hanging his laundry over the cooking stoves so it would dry faster.

Finally, he saved enough money to buy a Victorian house in a nice neighborhood in Sacramento. By then, my brother Chin and sister Wei, Ellen's mother, had already arrived in America. Wei had come as a bride and now lived with her husband and his family. Father then returned to China to make arrangements to move the rest of the family, a process that took more than a year. During that time in China, I was born; sixteen days earlier in America, Ellen was born.

Father, Mother, my sister Oi, and I arrived in America in 1950. My sister Esther was born in 1952. My parents had many adjustments to make, acquainting themselves with each other and at the same time raising children as older parents in a strikingly different American culture.

The cultural confusion was not much easier for my sisters and me. We had to try to fit in and figure out who we were, melding both Chinese and American ways and bridging a big generation gap. Esther and I went to American school in the daytime and Chinese school in the evenings. We spoke English at school and Chinese at home. It was easier in my younger years and more difficult in my teens. By the time I was sixteen, Father was seventy-six and his old-fashioned beliefs clashed with my independent ideas.

At a young age, Esther and I were fully aware of the mortality of our parents. Father was much older than most fathers and Mother had a near fatal stroke when I was only thirteen. We wanted to make the most of our time with them. Father loved to tell stories and we idolized him. As I grew older, our differences did not matter so much anymore. Mother's quiet strength made us feel loved and protected.

Father was proud when I graduated from college, the first of his children to do so. He died the next year in 1973, at eighty-four. Mother died six years later, at sixty-nine.

My parents taught us well about the importance of family. Perhaps because there had been a time when we were all separated, the idea of family seems even more precious to us. Father and Mother are no longer with me physically, but I often feel their presence.

On the Farm

ELLEN

I grew up in a family with five children, but it never seemed big compared with my father's family. His father had two wives under one roof and fourteen children in all in the tiny village of Hom Ha in southern China.

With few prospects at home, my father Lum Yip decided at age twenty to make his way to America to join a married sister on her farm in California. Earning $1.75 a day on the farm, it would take my father five years to repay his $2,000 passage money and save enough to return to China to seek a wife.

He soon met my mother Wei, who lived with her mother and siblings in a nearby village. At eighteen, she was considered old to be unmarried. Her own father was in America working and sending money whenever he could, but she had not seen him for many years.

At their marriage, my grandmother was happy that my mother would be reunited with her father, but at the same time heartbroken that once my mother left China for America, she might never see her again.

Fortunately, three years later, my grandfather was finally able to return to China to bring the rest of the family to America, including their infant daughter, my new aunt Annabel. We became fast friends immediately.

After ten years of working on leased land, my parents bought a sheep pasture in the Sacramento Valley that had been in the same family for over a hundred years. Our family had swelled to its final size, and we were grateful for the space in the property's large Victorian farmhouse despite its gloominess. The land included a scattering of dilapidated outbuildings, a barn, an outhouse, a chicken yard, a few trees, and little else. Our new neighbors were dubious about our prospects.

It took three years to transform the 240 acres from pasture to usable farmland. Wells were dug to replace inadequate windmills. Concrete pipe was laid to carry pumped water to the fields. Fuel pumps were installed for tractors and equipment. Eucalyptus trees were felled, and the soil was leveled, tilled, and enriched.

By the time my brothers' legs could reach the pedals, they were taught to

operate tractors and trucks.
We grew sugar beets, tomatoes, wheat, barley, field
corn, alfalfa, sorghum,
and beans.

In winter, sugar beets were
harvested by tractors that uprooted
the beets and sent them up a conveyer belt
to a truck alongside. Invariably, beets either
bounced off the conveyer belt onto the
ground or were missed entirely. On icy week-
end mornings, we were sent out to gather the
stray beets into piles and throw them one by
one into the truck someone drove from pile to
pile. Unlike a red beet, a sugar beet can weigh up
to ten or fifteen pounds. When we misjudged our
aim, beets slipped from our frozen hands to crash
into the side panels of the truck. Others were hurled
with too much energy and sailed over the truck
entirely. The largest beets required two of us to heave
them in together. We ducked from one another's
wilder efforts, then collapsed in laughter. By late morning, bored, hungry, and covered with flying dirt, we tor-
tured ourselves by guessing at the time and scanning the
horizon for my father's truck coming to take us home to a
well-deserved hot lunch.

Growing up, we learned about the weariness of long, hard hours and the
constant anxiety about capricious weather, but we also learned the satisfaction of
driving past row after row of flourishing crops and knowing we had played a
small part in feeding the world.

SUGAR BEET SIZE compared with RED BEET

COMFORT IN A BOWL: SOUP AND JOOK

In Chinese we say "drink soup" instead of "eat soup" as one says in English. This is because most Chinese soups (not including rice-based dishes like jook or congee, which is closer to a porridge) are broth based and seldom thickened, except perhaps with a little cornstarch. Pieces of meat, seafood, and/or vegetables, as well as noodles or wonton or other dumplings, give the soups flavor, add texture, and make them more substantive.

Most soups are served as a first course and are thought to possess cleansing or balancing properties. A large bowl of soup with a ladle is a fixture on many everyday dinner tables, allowing family members to serve themselves throughout the meal.

Hearty jooks and soups containing noodles or wonton are more commonly served on their own as a light but satisfying lunch rather than as part of a multicourse meal, the exception being Long-Life Noodle Soup, the final course at every special birthday banquet.

FAVORITE OLD STOCKPOT

Wonton

ELLEN

Making wonton was a family activity when I was growing up. We used to make at least 150 at a time. My mother patiently chopped the filling by hand, then called the children in to help with the wrapping. We quickly established a rhythm: scoop, roll, wet ends, fold. A carefully whittled chopstick with a flattened end, perfect for scooping the filling onto the corner of the wrappers, was a prized possession.

One by one we filled cookie sheets with wonton, neatly lined up and ready for boiling. Topped with a ladleful of chicken broth, the drained wonton made one of our favorite lunches.

Specially carved wonton chopstick

Wonton Soup

MAKES ABOUT 90 WONTON (8 TO 12 PER SERVING FOR A LUNCH ENTRÉE OR 4 TO 5 AS A FIRST COURSE)

To Annabel's father, a well-wrapped wonton looked like a little rosebud. The classic wonton fold is simple once you get the hang of it, but a common error is pinching the ends together at the wrong angle. Don't worry if you can't seem to get it right; by the time the wonton are boiled, it doesn't make much difference. If you keep a frozen supply of these, they can be boiled like ravioli, straight out of the freezer. Though we ate our wonton without toppings, there are many that you may add for color, texture, and heartiness. In China, sometimes even a spoonful of lard was stirred into the broth. Serve in a bowl of chicken broth and top with whatever vegetables you have on hand for a quick, satisfying meal or as a first course, although that is not traditional. Make up to 1 month ahead and freeze.

3–4	dried black mushrooms	OPTIONAL TOPPINGS	
2	green onions, cut into 1-inch pieces	1	carrot, cut in matchsticks
1	pound lean boneless pork, cut into 1-inch cubes	1	green onion, sliced thinly on the diagonal
1	pound medium shrimp, peeled and deveined	½	bunch spinach, leaves separated and washed thoroughly
1½	teaspoons salt	3–4	fresh mushrooms, sliced thinly
1	tablespoon soy sauce	¼	pound char siu (pages 136–137), cut in matchsticks
1	egg	¼	roast duck, cut into bite-sized pieces
2	1-pound packages wonton wrappers (These vary in thickness. You should have about 90 wrappers.)	1	cup cooked squid (page 96)
		1	cup cooked shrimp

TO SERVE

About ⅓ cup chicken broth per serving

Salt

CONDIMENTS

Soy sauce, sesame oil, hot chili oil, white pepper

Put the dried mushrooms in a small bowl with hot water to cover. Let stand 30 to 45 minutes to soften. Cut off and discard the hard stems, then rinse the caps and squeeze them dry. Chop the caps coarsely.

Combine the mushrooms, green onions, pork, shrimp, salt, soy sauce, and egg in a food processor. Pulse several times until the mixture is coarsely ground. (Alternatively, you can chop the mixture finely with a Chinese cleaver. Add the egg about halfway through chopping.) Transfer the mixture to a large shallow dish. To test that the mixture is seasoned to your taste, make a single wonton, boil it 5 minutes, taste, and adjust the seasoning. Never taste raw wonton filling.

To make the wonton, assemble: a cookie sheet, a teaspoon, a small bowlful of water, and a chopstick. Keep the unused wrappers under a damp towel as you work.

Place a wrapper on your left palm (if you are right-handed) with one corner at the tip of your middle finger. Using a chopstick, scoop about a teaspoon of filling off the edge of the plate onto that corner of the wrapper. Roll the wrapper from that corner toward you about halfway, until the filling is completely enclosed. Dip a chopstick into the water and wet the top of one of the rolled ends, then bring both rolled ends together, directly away from you, and pinch to seal. Set the finished wonton on cookie sheets as you work. (You may cover and freeze them at this point. Once they are frozen, transfer them to plastic bags.)

To serve, fill a large pot two-thirds full with water and bring to a boil. Meanwhile, prepare the optional toppings, if using. Bring the chicken broth to a

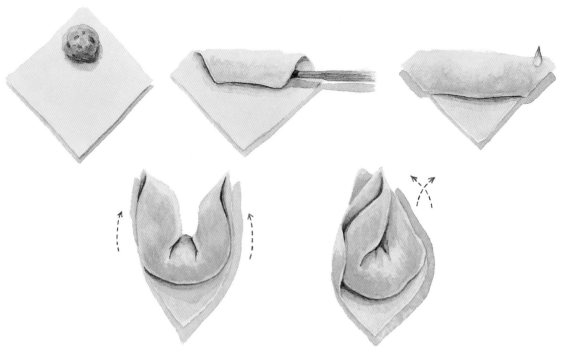

boil, then lower the heat to simmer. Add the salt to taste. When the water boils, drop about 15 to 20 wonton, one at a time, into the boiling water. Cook about 5 minutes, stirring very lightly with chopsticks to keep the wonton from sticking to the bottom of the pan; the wonton will float to the top when done. (Frozen wonton should be cooked a minute or two longer.) Test for doneness by cutting through the filling. It should not be raw looking or cold in the center.

Scoop out the wonton with a slotted spoon or wire mesh strainer. Rinse briefly under cool water to keep the wonton from sticking to one another, drain, and put into large individual bowls. Cook the next batches. Arrange the toppings over the wonton, if desired, then ladle enough hot chicken broth to almost cover the wonton. Serve with condiments on the side.

NOTE: Leftover filling may be frozen up to 3 weeks. Do not freeze wonton made with prefrozen filling. Leftover wrappers may be frozen for months, although they will lose some of their elasticity.

VARIATION

With Noodles: Add about 1 cup cooked lo mein noodles (or vermicelli) to each bowl before adding 5 to 8 wonton per person. Serve with broth, toppings, and condiments as above. Wonton over noodles are usually served as an entrée, not as a first course.

Simple Chicken Broth

Many Chinese pantries are stocked with canned chicken broth as a back-up. Homemade broth is more flavorful and almost as easy to have on hand if you make it ahead and freeze it. This version, made entirely without the usual vegetables or seasonings, allows the clean taste of chicken to come through and doesn't fight with other flavors in complex dishes.

3 pounds chicken backs and necks or 1 whole 3½- to 4½-pound chicken	3 quarts water

Wash the chicken pieces well and remove any spongy red material from the insides of the back pieces.

Put the chicken and water in a large stockpot, cover, and bring to a rolling boil. Immediately skim off any foam that has floated to the surface, reduce the heat to low, and simmer, covered, for 2½ hours. (If you are using a whole chicken, you may remove the chicken after the first 1½ hours and let it cool 20 minutes. Remove the skin and meat from the bones. Reserve the chicken meat for another use, return the bones and skin to the stockpot, and simmer 1 hour longer.) Uncover, increase the heat to medium, and cook 30 minutes longer.

Remove the chicken pieces with a slotted spoon or strainer and discard. Strain the broth through a fine sieve into a clean pot. Skim off all of the fat. (A fine wire mesh strainer works well. You may also refrigerate the broth overnight without skimming it and remove the hardened fat from the surface the next day.)

Taste the broth. If it tastes watery, bring to a boil and cook, uncovered, over medium heat for about 30 minutes, or until the broth is slightly reduced. Let cool. Do not salt the broth at this point. The amount of salt you need will depend on how the broth is used.

To freeze, measure the broth by ¼ cupfuls into muffin tins or by cupfuls into lidded plastic containers. When the broth in the muffin tins has frozen, set the tins in very hot water for a few seconds, invert the tins in a plastic bag, and shake out the frozen broth. Store frozen in the plastic bag and thaw as needed.

Refrigerated, the broth will keep about 3 days. Frozen, it will keep for several months.

Winter Melon Soup

For months after the harvest, Ellen's family stored basketball-sized winter melons in their hall closet. On special occasions, her parents would choose a winter melon that fit inside a stockpot and steamed the soup inside the melon itself. This simpler version does not require hours of steaming or such a large quantity of winter melon. You can make it as simple or elaborate as you wish, depending upon your choice of optional ingredients. Cut winter melon is available in some Asian grocery stores.

2–3 dried black mushrooms	2–3 fresh or canned water chestnuts, peeled if fresh, and minced
⅓ cup lotus seeds (optional)	
3–4 dried scallops (optional)	4 ounces cooked chicken or duck meat, shredded (optional)
1½ pounds winter melon (¾ pound after the rind is removed) (see Note)	4 ounces ham or char siu (pages 136–137), cut in matchsticks (optional)
5 cups unsalted chicken broth	
¼ cup bamboo shoots, cut in matchsticks	4 ounces crabmeat, picked over for shells (optional)
6 ounces prawns, peeled and deveined (optional)	Salt

Put the mushrooms in a small bowl with hot water to cover. Let stand 30 to 45 minutes to soften. Cut off and discard the hard stems. Rinse the caps, squeeze them dry, and cut into ⅛-inch-thick slices.

If using, put the lotus seeds in a small saucepan and cover with water. Soak for 40 minutes. Open the lotus seeds and discard the bitter dark green part inside. Bring the lotus seeds to a boil, then lower the heat and simmer until tender, about 20 minutes.

Put the dried scallops, if using, in a small bowl, and add just enough boiling water to cover. Let them stand 30 minutes. Reserve the soaking liquid and shred the scallops.

Cut off and discard the hard rind from the winter melon. Remove the seeds. Cut the flesh into ½-inch dice.

Bring the chicken broth to a boil. Add the mushrooms, lotus seeds, dried scallops and reserved soaking liquid, bamboo shoots, and winter melon. Lower the heat to medium-low and cook 15 minutes. Add the prawns and cook until they are pink and the winter melon is soft, about 5 minutes. Add the water chestnuts and chicken, ham or *char siu,* and crabmeat, if using, and heat through. Add the salt to taste.

THE HALL CLOSET AFTER
A WINTER MELON HARVEST

Watercress Soup

Watercress is considered *leung* (cooling), and supposedly cools the blood, making this a good soup to have after overindulgence in fried—or *ngit kui* (hot-breath)—foods. We had it often after parties.

1½ pounds pork neck bones or 1 pound country-style spareribs or pork shoulder

1 teaspoon salt, or to taste

6 cups water

12 small jujubes (Chinese red dates)

2 bunches watercress (5 ounces each)

Place the pork, salt, and water in a large saucepan. Cover and bring to a boil. With a spoon or fine-mesh sieve, skim off any fat or foam that rises to the surface. Rinse the jujubes and add them to the saucepan. Lower the heat and simmer, covered, for 1½ hours.

Meanwhile, wash the watercress and discard the large stems and any roots. You should have about 6 or 7 ounces of leafy stems remaining.

With a slotted spoon, remove the meat from the soup and set aside. Skim off any fat that has risen to the top of the broth, then add the watercress and simmer 10 minutes. While the watercress cooks, discard the bones from the meat and use 2 forks to shred the meat into bite-sized chunks, or cut the meat into chunks with a knife. Return the meat to the soup, heat through, and serve hot.

Noodles in Broth

Noodles in broth is a humble but praiseworthy dish. On a cold winter day, a big bowlful of noodles served in nourishing soup, embellished with favorite meat and vegetable toppings, warms the soul. Although this tastes best with fresh Chinese egg noodles, you can substitute dried Chinese noodles or even vermicelli if you take care not to overcook them.

NOODLE SEASONINGS

1 teaspoon peanut oil

¼ teaspoon sesame oil

1 teaspoon soy sauce

1 tablespoon oyster sauce

12 ounces fresh Chinese egg noodles, about ⅛ inch thick

4 cups Simple Chicken Broth (page 19) or low-sodium canned broth

1 cup sliced bok choy or other favorite vegetables, such as mushrooms, snow peas, or spinach, cut in bite-sized pieces

1 carrot, thinly sliced or cut in matchsticks

2 green onions, thinly sliced

2 tablespoons cilantro leaves

TOPPINGS

½ pound total, any combination of char siu (pages 136–137), ham, strips of cooked chicken or roast duck, or cooked prawns

CONDIMENTS

Soy sauce, oyster sauce, white pepper, sesame oil, hot chili oil

In a large bowl, mix together the noodle seasonings and set aside.

Fill a large saucepan two-thirds full with water, cover, and bring to a boil. Cook the noodles according to package instructions until just cooked through, about 5 minutes. Drain in a colander, rinse under cool water, and drain again.

Add the noodles to the bowl with the noodle seasonings and toss well to mix. Divide the noodles among 4 individual bowls and set aside.

Bring the chicken broth to a boil. Add the bok choy, carrot, and green onions and cook for about 2 minutes. Add the cilantro, then ladle over the noodles and garnish with the toppings. Serve with the condiments.

Long-Life Noodle Soup

This soup is traditionally served as the final course of a special birthday banquet. Although most guests will already have overindulged by this point, it is impolite not to have at least a small bowlful, as the long noodles represent long life. Guests endeavor to consume the soup without visibly biting off the noodles, which would symbolize cutting short the days left to the honoree. As children, this always seemed an important but nearly impossible challenge.

6–8 *dried black mushrooms*	1 *skinless, boneless chicken breast, cooked and cut in matchsticks (optional)*
8–12 *scallops*	
3 *cups water*	½ *cup yellow or green Chinese chives (see Note)*
8–12 *prawns, peeled and deveined (about ½ pound)*	2 *green onions, sliced thinly on the diagonal*
6 *ounces* char siu *(pages 136–137)*	2 *teaspoons oyster sauce, or to taste*
12 *snow peas*	1 *teaspoon sesame oil, or to taste*
6 *cups chicken broth*	
6 *ounces E-mein noodles (see Note)*	
8 *squid, cleaned and cooked (page 96) (optional)*	

Put the mushrooms in a small bowl with hot water to cover. Let stand 30 to 45 minutes to soften. When the mushrooms are soft, cut off and discard the hard stems. Rinse the caps, squeeze them dry, and slice thinly.

Halve the scallops, or quarter them if they are very large. Bring the water to a boil in a saucepan, add the scallops and prawns, and cook 1 minute, or until they are opaque white and cooked through. Drain the scallops and prawns and set aside.

Cut the *char siu* into matchstick-sized strips and reserve ¼ cup. Pinch off both ends from the snow peas and pull off the strings. Cut the snow peas diagonally if they are very large.

(If you are not using E-mein noodles, cook the noodles according to package instructions until just cooked; they should still be quite firm to the bite. Drain.)

In a saucepan, bring the chicken broth to a boil. Add the E-mein noodles and cook for about 2 minutes, until softened. Lower the heat to medium, add the mushrooms and snow peas, and cook 2 minutes longer. Stir in the squid, scallops, prawns, *char siu*, chicken breast, chives, and green onions and cook 15 seconds longer, just to heat through. Stir in the oyster sauce and sesame oil. Transfer the soup to a large serving bowl, top with the reserved *char siu*, and serve immediately.

NOTE: E-mein, also known as Yi mein or E-fu noodles, are puffy, partially pre-cooked egg noodles that hold their shape admirably in broth. If you cannot find them, you may substitute cooked linguine, but it will not have the same flavor or texture.

Yellow chives are available at some Asian markets. Like endive or white asparagus, they are "blanched," or protected from sunlight so that they do not turn green when they grow. You can substitute green Chinese chives or supermarket chives, but they will have a slightly different flavor.

Jook

Jook is Chinese comfort food, rice simmered with several times the normal amount of liquid until it has turned into a creamy, thick soup. At its most fundamental, jook is made with a ratio of one part rice to twelve parts canned low-sodium chicken broth; more elaborate versions incorporate everything from pork meatballs to a whole turkey carcass or barbecued pigs' feet. Jook is almost always accompanied by condiments and toppings—thin threads of ginger for bite, shredded lettuce for a contrasting crunch, and fresh cilantro leaves or sliced green onions for fragrance. Leftover jook thickens overnight in the refrigerator; add a little water to thin it before reheating.

chicken Jook

MAKES 8 SERVINGS

This is as comforting as any chicken soup we know.

1   3½- to 4½-pound chicken

13 cups water

1   tablespoon salt

1   cup rice

Optional Toppings and Condiments
(page 28)

Skin the chicken and leave whole. Combine the water and salt in a stockpot and bring to a boil. Add the chicken, lower the heat, and simmer, covered, for 50 minutes.

Remove the chicken and allow it to cool for 20 minutes. Meanwhile, skim the fat from the cooking liquid and add the rice. Shred the chicken or cut it into bite-sized chunks and set aside. Return the bones to the stockpot, bring the jook to a boil, then lower the heat, cover, and simmer for about 2 hours. Stir the jook occasionally to prevent it from sticking to the bottom of the stockpot.

Remove the bones from the jook. Stir the chicken meat into the jook during the last 5 minutes of cooking to heat through.

While the jook is cooking, put the toppings in separate small bowls. Ladle the hot jook into individual bowls and serve the toppings and condiments on the side.

VARIATION

Ground Pork Jook: Combine 1½ pounds ground pork, 4 teaspoons cornstarch, and 4 teaspoons soy sauce in a bowl and mix well. Form the mixture into small meatballs ½ inch in diameter. Fifteen minutes before the jook is done, add the meatballs and stir gently so they cook evenly. Add salt to taste.

vegetarian Jook

Jook is often served for breakfast in Chinese households and restaurants. This version may be for you if you like a meatless but hearty breakfast. It also makes a soothing, simple supper.

1   cup rice

5–6   ounces bean curd sticks (also called dried bean flour skins)

1   potato, peeled and cut into ½-inch dice

½   cup raw peanuts

3   quarts water

2   teaspoons salt, or to taste

OPTIONAL TOPPINGS

4–5   leaves romaine or iceberg lettuce, shredded

1   green onion, thinly sliced on the diagonal

1   1-inch piece ginger, peeled and cut in fine slivers

¼   cup roughly chopped cilantro leaves

CONDIMENTS

Sesame oil, hot chili oil, white pepper, soy sauce

Rinse and drain the rice. Break the bean curd sticks into 2- to 3-inch lengths and place in a stockpot with the potato, rice, peanuts, water, and salt.

Bring the jook to a boil, then lower the heat, cover, and simmer for about 1¾ to 2 hours. Stir the jook occasionally to prevent it from sticking to the bottom of the stockpot.

Put the toppings in separate small bowls.

When the jook is very thick and the rice is extremely creamy, serve hot in individual bowls, with the optional toppings and condiments on the side.

RAW PEANUTS

BEAN CURD STICKS

JOOK TOPPINGS

GINGER

ROMAINE
LETTUCE

CILANTRO

GREEN
ONION

Fish Jook

We sometimes prepare this dish by putting paper-thin slices of raw marinated fish into the bottom of individual bowls with a few condiments, then ladle hot jook over it; the heat of the jook is just enough to cook the fish to a delicate doneness. In the method below, the fish is a little more thoroughly cooked.

1 cup rice	1 tablespoon soy sauce
3 quarts Simple Chicken Broth (page 19) or canned low-sodium chicken broth	2 teaspoons dry sherry or rice wine
	1/2 teaspoon sesame oil
1 pound cod or snapper	Optional Toppings and Condiments (page 28)

Rinse and drain the rice. Place it in a stockpot with the broth and bring to a boil, then lower the heat, cover, and simmer for about 2 hours. Stir the jook occasionally to prevent it from sticking to the bottom of the stockpot

An hour before serving the jook, prepare the fish. With a very sharp knife, cut the fish crosswise into very thin slices, angling the knife diagonally across the grain. Carefully remove any bones. Place the fish in a bowl and toss with the soy sauce, dry sherry, and sesame oil.

While the jook is cooking, put the toppings in separate small bowls. Stir the fish into the jook during the last 10 minutes of cooking, gently separating the pieces of fish with a wooden spoon or chopsticks. Ladle the hot jook into individual bowls and serve with the toppings and condiments on the side.

VARIATION

Seafood Jook: Stir about 1/2 pound peeled deveined shrimp or cleaned squid or a combination of the two into the jook for the last 10 minutes of cooking. You can also make a third of the recipe for the meatballs in the Ground Pork Jook variation (page 27), and add them to the jook for the last 15 minutes of cooking.

Turkey Jook

MAKES 8 SERVINGS

For stomachs overstretched from a Thanksgiving feast, this tasty but mild meal made from the leftover turkey carcass is a soothing antidote. Note that the turkey carcass should be salted one day in advance.

Salt

1 whole turkey carcass

1–2 barbecued pigs' feet (optional)

14 cups water, or part water and part Simple Chicken Broth (page 19), or canned low-sodium chicken broth

1 cup rice

3 ounces bean curd sticks (also called dried bean flour skins)

1 potato, peeled and cut into ½-inch dice (optional)

½ cup raw peanuts (optional)

Optional Toppings and Condiments (page 28)

Sprinkle salt all over the turkey carcass. Cover and refrigerate overnight.

The next day, place the turkey carcass, pigs' feet, and water or water and chicken broth in a stockpot. Cover and bring to a boil, then lower the heat and simmer for 50 minutes, skimming off any fat or foam that rises to the surface.

Rinse and drain the rice. Break the bean curd sticks into 2- to 3-inch lengths and place in a stockpot with the rice, potato, and peanuts. Bring to a boil, lower the heat, cover, and simmer for 2 hours. Stir the jook occasionally to prevent it from sticking to the bottom of the stockpot.

Just before serving, remove the bones from the turkey and return the turkey meat to the stockpot. Add salt to taste. With a wooden spoon, break the pigs' feet into bite-sized chunks.

While the jook is cooking, put the toppings in separate small bowls. Ladle the hot jook into individual bowls and serve the toppings and condiments on the side.

Barbecued Pigs' Feet Jook

MAKES 8 SERVINGS

At the end of Ching Ming, when we sometimes take a whole Chinese barbecued pig to the cemetery to honor our ancestors, the pork is taken home and chopped up for a feast. This is what to do with the leftover pigs' feet the next day. You don't have to buy a whole pig just for an excuse to make this, however; barbecued pigs' feet are available at some Asian take-out markets.

4 barbecued pigs' feet (2½ to 3 pounds)

13 cups water

1 cup rice

2 teaspoons salt, or to taste

½ cup raw peanuts

Optional Toppings and Condiments (page 28)

Cut the pigs' feet in half at the joints. Put them in a large stockpot with the water, cover, and bring to a boil. Lower the heat and simmer 35 minutes, skimming off any fat or foam that rises to the surface.

Add the rice, salt, and peanuts, return to a boil, then lower the heat, cover, and simmer for 1¾ to 2 hours. Stir the jook occasionally to prevent it from sticking to the bottom of the stockpot. With a wooden spoon, break the meat into bite-sized chunks.

While the jook is cooking, put the toppings in separate small bowls. Ladle the hot jook into individual bowls and serve the toppings and condiments on the side.

RICE AND NOODLES

Every Chinese family we knew bought rice in fifty- or hundred-pound bags once or twice a year. The bags were made of burlap and were so big, most ended up in the corner of a bedroom or closet instead of the kitchen. No one saw the point of buying the rice sold in small boxes on supermarket shelves, since we would have needed a new box every day or two. The biggest mystery was Minute Rice, touted in commercials to cook in sixty seconds. No one saw the point of that either; what was the hurry?

The rhythm of rice being washed the traditional way is gentle and soothing. Cold water is added to a pot of raw rice, then one scoops up the rice and rubs it back and forth between the palms four or five times until it all falls back into the pot. This is repeated several times until the water turns cloudy and white. The water is drained off, fresh water is added, and the steps are repeated until the water stays almost clear. The music of rice being washed always reassured us that someone was thinking about our next meal.

Our mothers judged the ratio of rice to water by instinct and by checking that the water level reached one finger joint above the level of the raw rice. Perhaps the reputations different cooks earned for the hardness or softness of their rice had to do with the varying lengths of their fingers or which finger they chose to use.

Leftover rice was always steamed separately in a bowl, then stirred into the pot of finished rice. Since there was almost always a little rice left over, we used to imagine a grain of rice that escaped being eaten each time, traveling to successive pots for months on end.

Our parents repeated the superstition that the number of grains we left uneaten in our bowls or let fall on the table would foretell the number of freckles our future spouses would have. By this means, they taught us not to waste a single grain.

In addition to rice, the other staple starch is noodles. There are many types of Chinese noodles—egg noodles, wheat noodles, rice noodles, E-mein, and bean threads (also known as cellophane, long rice, and sai fun noodles); nearly all come in varying thicknesses and lengths. Egg, wheat, and rice noodles are sold fresh or dried, while the other noodles are only available dried. Fresh noodles freeze well.

Noodles are usually served as the only course for lunch. The exceptions are chow mein, which is sometimes served as one of the courses for a Chinese birthday lunch, and Long-Life Noodle Soup (page 24). Generally, rice and noodles are not served in the same meal; however, as Chinese families are becoming more Americanized, especially if they have young children who love chow mein, this rule is not always observed.

Our family uses fresh egg noodles, dried wheat noodles, fresh rice noodles, and, on occasion, E-mein. We love the variety and texture of noodles, and how they soak up the delicious sauces and flavors of other ingredients. When boiled and topped with stir-fried dishes like Oyster Beef with Broccoli (page 154) or Beef Stew variation (page 151), noodles make a nice alternative to rice. When pan-fried or oven-fried for chow mein, the noodles are crunchy on the outside and tender on the inside.

Cilantro

Steamed Rice

Rice for dinner was always washed just after lunch so it could soak for several hours before cooking. It does cook more evenly when soaked, but it's not always possible to be home at midday anymore. This version does not require soaking.

Many of us in the family now use rice cookers for convenience. They don't take up a burner and they turn off automatically at just the right moment, so you can't burn the rice accidentally. Still, rice cooked on the stovetop tastes just the tiniest bit better. We think it's worth the attention when you don't need to keep track of too many other dishes.

2   cups long-grain rice

Put the rice in a heavy saucepan. (A heavy saucepan is essential.) Cover the rice with cold water. Wash the rice by scooping it between your palms and rubbing it gently until it all falls back into the water. Repeat 3 or 4 times. You can also stir the rice with a wire whisk instead of using your hands, if you prefer.

Pour off the water, refill, and repeat the procedure 2 or 3 times, until the water stays almost clear after the rice has been washed. Pour off the water.

RICE COOKED ON THE STOVETOP TASTES JUST THE TINIEST BIT BETTER.

Add 3 cups of water. (If you want to do it the old way, check the water level by submerging your index finger to the top of the rice; the water should reach your first joint.)

Cover and bring the rice to a boil. Immediately lower the heat to simmer. To prevent the rice from boiling over, tip the lid slightly askew for about 30 seconds. Then cover tightly and cook 12 to 15 minutes, until all the water has been absorbed. Fluff the rice with a fork and let it rest a few minutes before serving.

Fried Rice

There is no definitive recipe for fried rice. The dish inspires creativity—all you need is rice and any ingredients you feel like adding; use a variety of vegetables and meats or one kind of each. As children, we were particularly fond of the country-style version made with pungent shrimp sauce, and that variation is included for those who share that memory.

- 4 cups cold cooked rice (leftover rice is perfect)
- ½–1 cup vegetables (such as green peas, sugar snap peas, snow peas, green beans, Chinese long beans, bok choy, celery, carrots, or zucchini)
- 2 eggs, lightly beaten
- 1 green onion, thinly sliced
- 1 cup cooked meat or seafood, cut into ½-inch dice, such as beef, pork, char siu (pages 136–137), ham, Chinese sausage, chicken, shrimp, crabmeat, or lobster
- 1 teaspoon plus 1 tablespoon vegetable or peanut oil

- 2 tablespoons chicken broth or water (optional)
- 4 teaspoons soy sauce, or to taste

Use your fingers or a fork to break up and separate the rice grains.

Cut the sugar snap peas, snow peas, celery, or bok choy diagonally into thin slices. Cut the green beans or Chinese long beans into ¼-inch lengths. Cut the carrots or zucchini in ¼-inch dice. Set aside.

Heat a nonstick skillet over medium heat, then heat 1 teaspoon oil. Add the eggs to the skillet, cook about 1 minute, turn them over, and let them set, about 1 minute longer. Remove the eggs to a plate, break apart into ½-inch pieces, and set aside.

Heat a wok over high heat, then heat 1 tablespoon oil. Add the green onion and meat or seafood and stir-fry about 2 minutes. Add the vegetables and stir-fry about 2 to 3 minutes. Add the rice and stir-fry about 2 to 3 minutes. If the rice seems dry, sprinkle 2 tablespoons chicken broth or water on the rice to moisten it.

Add the eggs and soy sauce and toss well. Serve immediately.

VARIATIONS

- **Vegetarian Fried Rice**: Omit the meat and increase the vegetables to 1 ½ to 2 cups.
- **Shrimp Fried Rice**: Substitute 1 cup raw, peeled, deveined shrimp cut in ½-inch pieces for the meat. Substitute 2 teaspoons shrimp sauce plus 1 teaspoon soy sauce for the soy sauce. (Shrimp sauce, or shrimp paste, tastes similar to anchovies; if you are trying it for the first time, you may want to add it sparingly.)

Fancy Present

ANNABEL

One Christmas after I had moved away from home, Mother told my sister Esther and me she had bought us each a wonderful present, one that we would really appreciate. Every time we spoke to her, she would allude to this great present, and all kinds of tantalizing visions swam in our heads—we knew we would not be getting the usual Christmas flannel pajamas. Esther said, "Maybe she bought us some fancy Chinese jewelry!" At last, Mother could no longer contain herself, and had to reveal that this stupendous gift was . . . a rice cooker!

After we got over our initial shock, my sister and I had a good laugh. But in the end I realized it *was* a wonderful gift. Every time I use the rice cooker, I think of Mother and I smile.

Sticky Rice with Sausage and Taro Root

MAKES 6 TO 8 SERVINGS AS PART OF A CHINESE MEAL

This is a favorite at our Thanksgiving gatherings. It can even be used as a stuffing. However, we usually have it as a side dish next to our turkey. Some second-generation Chinese call this "Special Rice." Recipes from other villages may include minced pork, minced chicken, and fresh or dried shrimp.

2½ cups glutinous rice (also called sweet rice)	1½ cups water
Salt	1½ cups taro root (about ½ pound, unpeeled)
2 Chinese sausages, cut into ¼-inch dice (or ½ cup diced ham)	1 green onion, thinly sliced
3–4 dried black mushrooms	3–4 Chinese black olives, pitted and coarsely chopped (optional) (see Note)
1 ounce dried shrimp (optional)	Soy sauce (optional)
1 teaspoon vegetable or peanut oil	

In a large bowl, wash and drain the rice. Add 1 teaspoon salt and enough water to cover by ¼ inch. Soak for 2 hours.

In a nonstick skillet over medium heat, stir-fry the Chinese sausages until lightly browned and slightly crisp, about 3 minutes. Drain on several layers of paper towels.

Put the mushrooms in a small bowl with hot water to cover. Let stand 30 to 45 minutes to soften. Cut off and discard the hard stems. Rinse the caps, squeeze them dry, and cut into ¼-inch dice.

Larger variety is firmer
TARO
Small variety is lighter-textured

Pick over the dried shrimp. Rinse, then cover them with cold water and let stand 30 minutes to soften. Drain.

Set a rack in a large pot and add water to a depth of 1½ to 2 inches. (If you are using a steamer, fill the lower tier with water.) Bring to a boil. Oil a 2-quart heatproof bowl. Drain the rice thoroughly and put it in the bowl with 1½ cups water and ½ teaspoon salt. (Drain the rice and measure the water carefully; too much water will make the rice mushy.) Set the bowl on the rack (or on the upper tier of the steamer), cover, and steam over high heat for 45 minutes, replenishing the pot with boiling water as necessary.

Meanwhile, peel and cut the taro root into ½-inch dice. Wear rubber dishwashing gloves to protect your hands; raw taro root may cause your hands to itch. Place the taro root in a saucepan with ¼ teaspoon salt and enough water to cover. Bring to a boil, lower the heat, and simmer until tender, 7 to 8 minutes. Drain and allow to cool.

In the skillet, stir-fry the Chinese sausages or ham with the dried shrimp, green onion, black mushrooms, and olives for 1 minute over medium heat. Turn the rice out into a large bowl and gently mix in the sausage mixture and cooked taro root. Add salt or soy sauce to taste. Serve hot.

NOTE: Chinese black olives are very salty and strongly flavored. If you are trying these olives for the first time, you may want to use them sparingly. Do not substitute other olives.

Jeng

ELLEN

When my mother left China as a newlywed, my grandmother had no assurance that she would ever see her again. She worried whether my mother would have adequate food and a comfortable new home in America. When my mother did arrive in her new home, she hastily wrote to reassure my grandmother everything was fine, giving two examples of her good fortune: First, in America she could start a stove with the simple turn of a knob. Second, *jeng* was made year-round, not just for the two special festivals at which they were served in China.

Jeng are bamboo-leaf-wrapped packets of sweet rice studded with bits of pork, preserved egg yolk, and other savory morsels. I made hundreds of *jeng* with my mother when I was young. Assembling the packets was an elaborate process that required four hands: one person held the bamboo leaf cone in place while the other added the filling, finished the folding, and tied the packet with string. The *jeng* were then placed in enormous kettles that had to be replenished with boiling water throughout the seven-hour cooking time. They seemed like something I could never make on my own.

Only when Annabel and I began to write this book did we resolve to attempt this recipe. I washed ten pounds of rice and scrubbed and boiled over a hundred bamboo leaves. Early the next morning, Annabel arrived loaded with enthusiasm and ingredients I had forgotten. We extracted two dozen preserved egg yolks, peeled chestnuts, and diced salt pork. I found some antique hatpins to pin the bamboo leaves together. We reviewed our detailed notes over coffee and scones.

Confidently, I fished the first bamboo leaves out of the kettle to form a cone for the rice, only to realize I had forgotten the special fold.

Making the packets just right is critical, because if the leaves are folded incorrectly, the finished *jeng* will be lopsided. Worse, rice may leak out during cooking. In desperation we called my mother, who tried unsuccessfully to explain the exact technique over the phone.

We worked clumsily through much of the afternoon, folding and tying dozens of misshapen packets. Annabel finally left, loaded with half the *jeng* to boil at home. I put the rest on the stove and tended them for seven hours.

Very late that evening, I pulled my first *jeng* out of the steaming pot. It had magically become plump from the expanding rice. When I opened the leaves, a rich bamboo scent rose from the glistening sweet rice, which looked just as I remembered. The first bite erased all traces of my exhaustion.

We've since gotten hands-on instruction on forming the folds properly and developed a simplified version that can be made without a partner, and that doesn't require such a gargantuan appetite for sweet rice.

Savory Jeng

MAKES ABOUT 20 *JENG*

Even a small batch of the traditional large *jeng* was too much for a small family, so we've devised a more manageable version. There are many optional fillings, of which we've listed a few, but the *jeng* are delicious without these additions. Try adding a few hard-cooked eggs to discover how wonderfully bamboo enhances their flavor. These freeze well.

100	*dried bamboo leaves (see Note)*
5	*pounds glutinous rice (also called sweet rice)*
	Salt
20	*salted preserved duck eggs (page 47)*
1½	*pounds barbecued pork, salt pork, or Chinese sausage, or a combination*
	Cotton string
	Hard-cooked eggs (optional)

OPTIONAL FILLINGS

1	*cup adzuki beans, soaked overnight, then drained and mixed with ½ teaspoon salt*
	About ½ cup raw peanuts
20–40	*dried chestnuts, soaked in hot water for 30 minutes*
⅓	*cup dried shrimp, soaked in cold water 30 minutes (cut in 2 to 3 pieces if large)*

The day before making the *jeng*, fill a sink with very hot water. Soak the bamboo leaves until they are soft and somewhat pliable, about 30 minutes. Rinse them in 3 changes of hot water to remove any grit. Place the leaves in a large pot, fitting

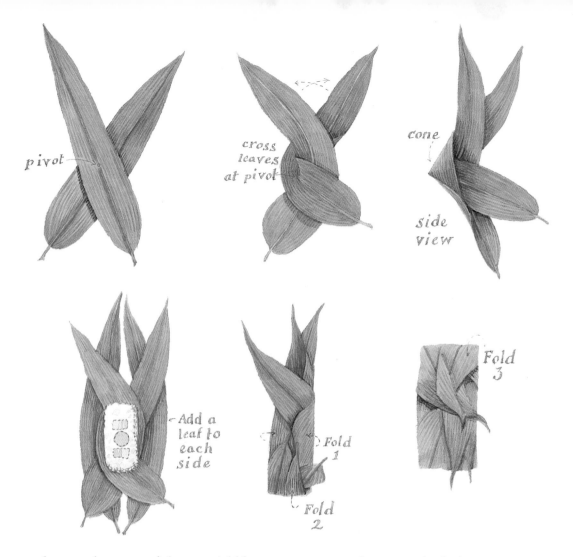

them to the curve of the pot. Add hot water to cover, bring to a boil, then remove from the heat and let the leaves stand, covered, overnight. (This is an important step because the leaves must be made as pliable as possible or they will split when they are folded.)

Wash the rice, drain, cover with water, and let stand at least 2 hours or overnight. Drain. Stir in 2 to 3 tablespoons salt.

Crack the salted preserved duck eggs one at a time into a small bowl. Pick out the yolk, discarding the whites, and rinse it off under cold water. The yolks should be firm and bright orange, and the eggs should have a briny odor. If a yolk is soft and mustard-colored or the white is gray or black and has a strong odor, the egg has spoiled and should be discarded. Set the rinsed yolks aside in another bowl.

Trim the barbecued pork or salt pork into 1 × ¾ × ¾-inch pieces or cut the

Chinese sausages into 1-inch lengths. (You will need 2 pieces of meat per *jeng*, about 40 pieces in all.)

Hold one leaf in your left palm, vein side down, with the stem end pointing toward your wrist. Lay a second leaf, vein side down, diagonally over the first leaf (see illustration). Grasp the leaves with your thumbs and forefingers from both sides of the intersection, then cross the leaf tips over at that pivot point to form a cone. Cup the cone in one palm, then lay a leaf, vein side out, along each side as shown.

Scoop a scant ¼ cup raw rice into the bottom of the cone. (If desired, you can mix the soaked beans into the rice before scooping into the cone.) Center a piece of yolk on this, then add a piece of meat or sausage on either side of the yolk. (You may scatter some peanuts or dried shrimp over this, if using, or place a chestnut or two next to the meat.) Scoop another ½ cup rice over the other ingredients to cover.

Fold the side leaves over to cover the rice (fold 1). Fold the stem ends away from you and hold them down with your thumb (fold 2), then fold the leaf tips toward you and hold them down with your thumb (fold 3).

Grasp the end of a ball of string under your thumb and wind the string cross-wise around both ends of the *jeng* 2 or 3 times You must keep the string somewhat loose to allow the rice to expand while cooking. Cut the string and knot the ends together securely.

Put all the *jeng* in a large kettle and add water to cover. Bring to a boil and cook over high heat for 5 hours, replenishing the pot with boiling water as necessary to keep the *jeng* covered with water. If desired, add several hard-cooked eggs to the *jeng* during the last 2 or 3 hours of cooking. The whites will take on a beige tint and the eggs will be subtly flavored by the bamboo leaves.

When the packets have swelled and the rice is tender, drain the *jeng*. (*Jeng* may be made several days ahead and refrigerated for 3 days or frozen. To reheat, thaw if frozen, then boil for 15 to 20 minutes.)

To serve, unwrap the hot *jeng*. Cut it in half crosswise, then cut each piece crosswise again, so that you have 4 pieces altogether. Each *jeng* serves 2.

NOTE: One 14-ounce package of leaves contains over 200 leaves. You will only need about 80 leaves, especially if they are very large. However, you must have extra on hand in case a leaf splits. Unused leaves can be air-dried for reuse.

Sweet Jeng

Actual Size—Soo Mook

The addition of potassium carbonate to this recipe softens the rice and gives it an interesting yellow color and subtle flavor. Slivers of *soo mook* wood add their own mild flavor and turn the center part of the *jeng* beet red, making this a colorful, delicious treat. The leaves must be boiled a day before you plan to use them.

18–24 dried bamboo leaves (see Note, page 43)

3 cups glutinous rice (also called sweet rice)

4 teaspoons gan jui (potassium carbonate solution)

3 or 4 pieces soo mook *wood (optional)*

Cotton string

Maple syrup, corn syrup, or sugar

The day before making the *jeng*, fill a sink with very hot water. Soak the bamboo leaves until they are soft and somewhat pliable, about 30 minutes. Rinse them in 3 changes of hot water to remove any grit, then place the leaves in a large pot, fitting them to the curve of the pot. Add hot water to cover and bring to a boil. Turn off the heat and let the leaves stand, covered, overnight. (This is an important step because the leaves must be made as pliable as possible or they will split when they are folded.)

Wash the rice in a bowl, drain, and add water to cover. Let stand overnight. Drain. Add the *gan jui* and blend until the rice is an even, yellowish color.

With a sharp knife, carefully break the pieces of *soo mook* into 9 slivers, each slightly larger than a matchstick. (Pieces of wood that are too large will cause the *jeng* to turn too red and impart a bitter flavor.)

Remove 2 bamboo leaves from the water. Lay them slightly overlapping lengthwise, vein side down, across your palm. Distribute ½ cup rice evenly lengthwise down the middle 6 inches of the leaves, leaving a 1-inch margin at the sides. Bury a sliver of wood lengthwise in the middle of the rice.

Fold the sides up over the top to cover the rice, then fold the ends up over the middle. Hold the *jeng* closed firmly under your thumb. Put the end of a string under your thumb and wind the string around the leaves crosswise 7 or 8 times loosely enough to allow the rice to expand while cooking. Cut the string and knot the ends together securely.

Place the *jeng* in a large pot. Cover them with water, bring to a boil, and cook over high heat for 2½ hours, replenishing the pot with boiling water as necessary. Remove the *jeng* from the pot. (*Jeng* may be made several days ahead and refrigerated, or frozen for 2 to 3 months. Thaw, then reheat by boiling 10 minutes.)

Unwrap the *jeng*. Cut it in half crosswise and remove the wood sliver. Cut each piece of *jeng* crosswise again, so that you have 4 pieces altogether. Serve hot or at room temperature with maple syrup, corn syrup, or a dish of sugar for dipping. Allow 1 *jeng* per person.

About Eggs

When we think of eggs now, we rarely think beyond the innocuous chicken eggs nestled safely in their cardboard carton in the refrigerator.

Growing up, however, eggs suggested many enticing possibilities. They might be salted preserved duck eggs floating in a jar of tea-colored brine, festive red-dyed eggs, pickled eggs with pigs' feet, or eggs whose whites had acquired a subtle scent of bamboo from hours of simmering in a potful of boiling *jeng.*

To the uninitiated, the most unusual eggs are *pi don*, preserved in a dark coating of mysterious clay. With their translucent, obsidian-colored "whites" and creamy gray-green yolks, they are an acquired taste, indescribably delicious paired with a bit of pickled ginger, pickled shallots, or stirred into a bowlful of steaming jook.

In our homes, even a simple fried egg served over rice had a fanciful name, *boh bao don,* "wallet egg," because it resembled a kind of Chinese wallet one wore around one's waist, complete with a piece of gold inside. With a dab of oyster sauce and a sprinkling of chopped green onion, this made a wonderful simple dish for a dinner short on courses.

HOH BAO DON

PI DON

PICKLED EGG

RED~DYED EGG
for New Baby Party

JENG EGG

PRESERVED SALTED
EGG YOLK

Salted Preserved Eggs

MAKES 2 DOZEN EGGS

Salted preserved duck eggs are available at some Asian markets, but they are not difficult to make if you can't find them or you want to try preserving your own. However, they must cure for at least one month before using. The tea gives the egg yolks an oilier texture and richer color. Salted eggs can be boiled, peeled, and quartered as a side dish to accompany Steamed Rice (page 35) or jook (see page 26); they can also be used as an ingredient in recipes such as Savory *Jeng* (page 41) or Steamed Minced Pork (page 139).

3 cups pickling salt

1 tablespoon black tea leaves, such as oolong (optional)

8 cups water

2 dozen large chicken or duck eggs

Bring the salt, tea leaves, and water to a boil. Remove from the heat and cool completely.

Put the eggs in a large crock or glass jar. Add the cooled brine to cover them. Place a plate over the top of the crock or jar and set it in a dark, cool place for a month.

Remove an egg, rinse it, and put it in a saucepan with enough water to cover it. Bring to a boil over medium heat, lower the heat, and simmer for 7 to 8 minutes. When the egg is cooled, peel it and taste to see if the egg has the desired saltiness. If not, let the remaining eggs stand in the brine up to 7 days longer.

Remove the eggs from the brine and store, refrigerated, up to a month. Even if the whites have become too salty and are no longer palatable as a side dish, the yolks will still be usable for other recipes.

Stir-Fried Rice Noodles (Chow Fun)

MAKES 4 TO 6 SERVINGS

Many Asian markets sell tender fresh rice noodles. Their flavor and texture differ considerably from wheat-based noodles. They are fully cooked, so a brief reheating is all they need; overcooking will make them sticky.

12 ounces flank steak

MARINADE
2½ teaspoons soy sauce
⅛ teaspoon sugar
1 teaspoon dry sherry or rice wine

1½ pounds fresh rice noodles

NOODLE SEASONINGS
1 tablespoon soy sauce
½ teaspoon salt
½ teaspoon sugar
¼ teaspoon white pepper

1–2 tablespoons vegetable or peanut oil
1 medium yellow onion, halved and thinly sliced
3 ounces Chinese chives or 3 green onions, cut into 1-inch pieces
2 cups bean sprouts (optional)
¾ cup chicken broth
   Oyster sauce
2½ teaspoons cornstarch mixed with ¼ cup cold water or chicken broth

Cut the flank steak diagonally across the grain into ⅛-inch slices. (This is easier if you freeze the meat about 30 minutes, until firm but not frozen hard, just before slicing it.) Combine the marinade ingredients in a medium bowl and add the flank steak. Marinate for at least 30 minutes and up to 2 hours.

Unless they are very fresh and pliable, put the noodles in a heatproof dish for steaming. Set a rack in a pot and add water to a depth of 1½ to 2 inches. (If you are using a steamer, fill the lower tier half full with water.) Bring to a boil. Set the dish on the rack (or on the upper tier of the steamer) and steam over high heat until just heated through, about 10 minutes. Remove from the pot, cover loosely with foil, and keep warm.

Combine the soy sauce, salt, sugar, and white pepper for the noodle seasonings in a small bowl and set aside.

Place a wok over medium-high heat. Heat 1 tablespoon of oil, then add the flank steak and stir-fry until browned, about 4 minutes. Remove and keep warm. Add more oil to the wok if necessary, then add the onion and stir-fry until soft and transparent, about 4 minutes. Add the chives or green onions, bean sprouts, and noodle seasonings and cook 30 seconds. Return the meat to the wok, add the chicken broth, and heat through. Add the oyster sauce to taste.

Stir in the cornstarch mixture and cook until the sauce has thickened. Then add the noodles and toss gently to distribute the sauce evenly and heat through. Serve immediately.

NOTE: Rice noodles are sold in 2-pound packages in many Asian markets. The form we recommend are precut about ½ inch wide, or you may buy them uncut and cut them ½ inch wide before steaming them. Do not use thin tender rice noodles for this recipe.

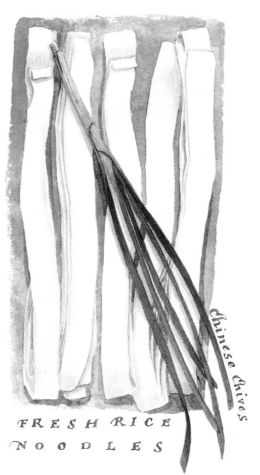

FRESH RICE NOODLES

Chinese Chives

VARIATIONS

+ **With Char Siu:** Substitute 12 ounces *char siu* (pages 136–137) (you do not need to marinate it), cut into ⅛-inch diagonal slices, for the flank steak.
+ **With Chicken:** Substitute 12 ounces skinless, boneless chicken, cut into bite-sized pieces, for the flank steak. Marinate and cook as for flank steak, but stir-fry about 6 minutes.

Tomato Beef Chow Mein

MAKES 4 TO 6 SERVINGS

Many of our homegrown tomatoes went into this lunch favorite. Here we use the oven method to "fry" the noodles, which uses less oil, but see the Note if you prefer the more authentic pan-fried version.

2 pounds fresh tomatoes, peeled, or 1 28-ounce can unseasoned whole tomatoes

2–3 tablespoons sugar, or to taste

1 pound flank steak

1 tablespoon soy sauce

⅛ teaspoon sugar

1½ teaspoons dry sherry or rice wine

2 tablespoons peanut oil

1 12-ounce package fresh Chinese chow mein noodles (see Note)

1 yellow onion, quartered

2 celery stalks, thinly sliced

1 bell pepper, seeded and cut into 1-inch squares

1 fresh tomato, cut in 8 wedges

Salt

Cut the tomatoes into eighths if large or quarters if smaller and place in a saucepan. Cook, uncovered, over low heat for 20 minutes. (If you are using canned tomatoes, measure 2 cups of tomatoes, dice them, place them in a saucepan, and heat through.) Add 2 to 3 tablespoons sugar to balance the tartness of the tomatoes. Remove from the heat and set aside.

Slice the flank steak diagonally across the grain into ⅛-inch-thick slices and then into pieces 3 inches long. (This is easier if you freeze the meat about 30 minutes, until firm but not frozen hard, just before cutting it.) Combine the soy sauce, sugar, and dry sherry in a medium bowl and add the flank steak. Marinate for at least 30 minutes and up to 2 hours.

Cook the noodles according to package instructions, until barely cooked through. Drain in a colander, rinse under cool water, and drain again.

Line a cookie sheet with aluminum foil and spread 1 tablespoon oil evenly over the foil. Arrange the drained noodles on the foil in an even layer and bake the noodles 10 to 15 minutes, until they are slightly crispy. Lower the heat to 400°F., turn the noodles to the other side, and cook 10 minutes longer. Set aside.

Place a wok over high heat. Heat 1 tablespoon of oil, then add the onion, celery, and pepper. Stir-fry until the onion is soft and transparent, about 4 minutes. Remove the vegetables from the wok. Add 1 tablespoon oil to the wok, then stir-fry the flank steak until browned and any liquid has evaporated, about 4 minutes.

Add the tomato mixture and cut-up fresh tomato and heat through. Add salt to taste. Add the noodles and toss to coat evenly. Serve immediately.

NOTE: If fresh chow mein noodles are not available, you may substitute 9 ounces dried chow mein noodles or vermicelli cooked according to package instructions. You do not need to fry or bake the vermicelli.

The chow mein noodles can also be fried. This method is more authentic but requires more oil and more attention: Divide the drained noodles into 3 portions. Heat a skillet over high heat, then heat 1 to 2 tablespoons oil. Add 1 portion of noodles and cook until the underside is light golden brown, about 2 to 3 minutes. Turn the noodles over and cook until the second side is light golden brown, about 2 minutes. Reduce the heat slightly if the noodles are browning too quickly. Keep the finished noodles warm in a 200°F. oven, loosely covered with aluminum foil. Repeat the procedure with the remaining portions, adding 1 to 2 tablespoons oil to the pan each time.

vegetarian Chow Mein

MAKES 4 TO 6 SERVINGS

This is a variation on Uncle Bill's Chow Mein (page 54) for those who want a vegetarian alternative. You may experiment with different vegetables, such as chard, spinach, bell peppers, or yellow onions.

8   dried black mushrooms

3   ounces dried bean curd sticks (also called dried bean flour skins)

1   10-ounce package firm tofu

3   tablespoons plus 2 teaspoons peanut oil

½   teaspoon sugar

1½ teaspoons dark soy sauce plus 1½ teaspoons light soy sauce (or 1 tablespoon Kikkoman soy sauce)

1½ teaspoons dry sherry or rice wine

½   teaspoon salt

⅛   teaspoon pepper

2   eggs, lightly beaten

1   12-ounce package fresh Chinese chow mein noodles (see Note)

1   garlic clove, finely chopped

1   celery stalk, thinly sliced

4   ounces snow peas, strings removed

2   ounces fresh mushrooms, thinly sliced

1   carrot, cut in matchsticks

1¾ cups vegetable stock (see Note) or canned vegetable broth

4–6 leaves napa cabbage, shredded

4–6 fresh water chestnuts, peeled and sliced

½   pound bean sprouts

2   green onions, thinly sliced

Put the black mushrooms in a small bowl with hot water to cover. Let stand 30 to 45 minutes to soften.

Break the bean curd sticks into 2-inch lengths. Soak 30 minutes in enough hot water to cover. Place the bean curd sticks and soaking water in a small saucepan and simmer about 10 minutes to soften. Drain.

Cut the tofu into ½ × ¼ × 1½-inch pieces. Place a nonstick skillet over medium-high heat and heat 1 tablespoon oil. Add the tofu. Turn to brown lightly on all sides, 5 to 6 minutes. Set aside.

Mix the sugar, soy sauce, dry sherry, salt, and pepper in a small bowl and set aside.

When the black mushrooms have softened, cut off and discard the hard stems. Rinse the caps and squeeze them dry. Cut the mushrooms into ¼-inch-thick slices.

Place a nonstick skillet over medium heat and heat 2 teaspoons oil. Swirl the skillet so the oil coats the bottom well. Pour the eggs into the skillet and cook until just set. Turn the eggs and cook on the second side until just set. Transfer to a platter and let cool for 5 minutes. Roll the eggs up, cut into ¼-inch strips, and set aside.

Prepare the noodles as for Tomato Beef Chow Mein (page 50), using either the "frying" method in the oven or the pan-fried method (see Note, page 51).

Place a wok over high heat and heat 1 tablespoon oil. Add the garlic and stir-fry for a few seconds. Add the soy sauce mixture with the celery, snow peas, fresh mushrooms, black mushrooms, and carrot with about ½ cup of the vegetable stock. Stir-fry until the vegetables are crisp-tender, about 2 minutes.

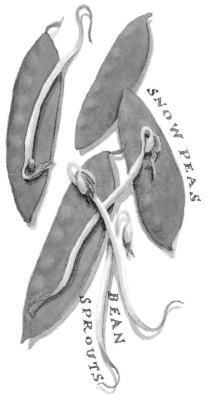

Add the bean curd sticks, tofu, napa cabbage, and the remaining 1¼ cups vegetable stock and stir-fry 1 minute. Add the noodles, breaking them up with a spatula. Mix them well into the other ingredients and cook 1 to 2 minutes, or until most of the liquid has been absorbed. Add the water chestnuts and bean sprouts and stir-fry 30 seconds. Finally, mix in the green onions and eggs, add more soy sauce to taste, and serve immediately.

NOTE: If fresh chow mein noodles are not available, you may substitute 9 ounces dried chow mein noodles or vermicelli cooked according to package instructions. You do not need to fry or bake the vermicelli.

To make vegetable stock: Combine 3 celery stalks and a quartered onion with 3 cups water and 8 peppercorns in a large saucepan and bring to a boil. Lower the heat and simmer 45 minutes. Uncover, bring to a boil, and continue to cook, uncovered, 15 minutes longer to reduce the liquid. Strain the stock through a sieve and discard the vegetables. You should have 1¾ to 2 cups stock.

Uncle Bill's Chow Mein

Uncle Bill is one of the best cooks in the family. Before he retired, he owned a grocery store. In the dimly lit back of the store, alongside crates of Coca-Cola, cartons of penny candy, and an old vinyl easy chair was a well-used Wedgewood stove. Next to the stove was a shelf holding bottles of soy sauce and sherry and a few jars of spices. From that stove and those simple ingredients, Uncle Bill created many memorable meals. His chow mein is a classic and no family party is complete without it.

8 *dried black mushrooms*	1 *garlic clove, finely chopped*
½ *pound boneless chicken breast or thigh meat*	1 *cup sliced bok choy, cut 1-inch thick on the diagonal*
½ *pound* char siu *(pages 136–137) (or ham)*	1 *celery stalk, thinly sliced on the diagonal*
½ *teaspoon sugar*	1 *carrot, cut in matchsticks*
1½ *teaspoons dark soy sauce plus 1½ teaspoons light soy sauce (or 1 tablespoon Kikkoman soy sauce)*	4 *ounces snow peas, strings removed*
	2 *ounces fresh mushrooms, sliced*
1½ *teaspoons dry sherry or rice wine*	*About 2 cups chicken broth*
½ *teaspoon salt*	1 *teaspoon cornstarch mixed with 2 teaspoons cold water or chicken broth*
⅛ *teaspoon pepper*	
1 *12-ounce package fresh Chinese chow mein noodles (see Note, page 51)*	½ *pound bean sprouts*
	2 *green onions, thinly sliced on the diagonal*
2 *tablespoons peanut oil*	2 *tablespoons oyster sauce*

Put the black mushrooms in a small bowl with hot water to cover. Let stand 30 to 45 minutes to soften.

Cut the chicken into ¼ × ¼ × 1½-inch strips. Cut the *char siu* into ¼-inch-thick slices (or cut the ham into ¼ × ¼ × 1½-inch strips). Set aside in separate bowls.

Combine the sugar, soy sauce, dry sherry, salt, and pepper and set aside.

When the black mushrooms have softened, cut off and discard the hard stems. Rinse the caps and squeeze them dry. Cut the mushrooms into ¼-inch-thick slices.

Preheat the oven to 425°F.

Prepare the noodles as for Tomato Beef Chow Mein (page 50), using either the "frying" method in the oven or the pan-fried method (see Note, page 51).

Place a wok over high heat and heat the remaining tablespoon of oil. Add the garlic and chicken and stir-fry 30 seconds. Stir in the soy sauce mixture, then add the bok choy, celery, carrot, snow peas, fresh mushrooms, and black mushrooms. Add about ½ cup chicken broth and stir-fry until the vegetables are crisp-tender, about 2 minutes.

Add the *char siu* or ham and 1¼ cups chicken broth and stir-fry for 1 minute. Add the noodles, breaking them up with a spatula. Cook together with the other ingredients for 1 to 2 minutes, or until most of the liquid has been absorbed. Add another ¼ cup chicken broth if there is not enough liquid left for a sauce. Push the noodles to one side and stir the cornstarch mixture into the remaining liquid, cooking over medium-high heat until the sauce has thickened. Add the bean sprouts and stir-fry 30 seconds. Mix in the green onions and oyster sauce and serve immediately.

Noise

ELLEN

Some people perceive us Chinese as polite and quiet, but I remember raucous and noisy conversations that sounded like shouted arguments as everyone spoke at once. As children, we winced at amicable but clamorous discussions between my parents and grandparents, especially when they took place in a car with all the windows rolled up. Other times, my father drove and sang Chinese opera at the top of his voice along with a cassette full of clashing cymbals and gongs.

In mah-jongg, players slammed down worthless tiles with exasperated oaths or punctuated the game's progress with exclamations of triumph at their cleverness or luck. They loudly lamented their miscalculations or shared their astute guesses over the sharp clacking of tiles being scrambled for the next hand.

In contrast, dinner conversation was quite subdued. I used to try to initiate conversations, to be more like the sitcom families I saw on TV, but I was not very successful. I was relieved to find that my family was not socially inept when I read years later that conversation at a Chinese dinner table is considered an almost rude intrusion on the serious business of eating.

DIM SUM

Some of the translations for "dim sum" are "heart's delight," "touch your heart," and "a little bit of heart." Dim sum includes an amazing assortment of small dishes and snacks that are enjoyed in restaurants and occasionally in homes.

For the uninitiated, we highly recommend a trip to a dim sum restaurant, where customers are surrounded by bustling waiters and waitresses pushing carts full of morsels from which customers select whatever suits their fancy: *char siu bao* (buns filled with barbecue pork), *ha gow* and *siu mai* (stuffed savory dumplings), egg rolls, pot stickers, bite-sized portions of pork spareribs, stuffed bell peppers, *lek doi* (Chinese doughnuts), curried meat pastries, chicken in foil, dry-fried prawns, deep-fried taro root turnovers, beef meatballs on spinach beds, shrimp toast, and *don tot* (custard tarts) are only a sampling of what is offered. The dim sum are served with a variety of savory, sweet, spicy, or hot dips. (See the Sweets chapter on page 173 for additional recipes.)

Few people take time now to make dim sum, but women in our family used to gather to socialize and make hundreds of those treats at a time. We hope you'll try making them with your friends, too.

Ha Gow

In dim sum restaurants, *ha gow* are single bites filled with shrimp and some bamboo shoots. The *ha gow* we used to make (see illustration, page 57) also included pork, water chestnuts, and black mushrooms and couldn't be eaten politely in just one bite.

FILLING
- 2–3 black mushrooms
- 4 ounces pork shoulder (not too lean), cut into 1-inch cubes
- 5 ounces shrimp, peeled and deveined
- 2–3 fresh or canned water chestnuts, peeled if fresh, and sliced
- 2 ounces bamboo shoots, sliced
- 1/4 teaspoon sugar
- 1/4 teaspoon salt
- 1/8 teaspoon white pepper
- Few drops of sesame oil
- 1 teaspoon vegetable or peanut oil
- 1 teaspoon cornstarch mixed with 1 tablespoon water

DOUGH
- 2 cups wheat starch
- 1 1/2 cups boiling water

CONDIMENTS
- 2 teaspoons Coleman's Hot Mustard mixed with 1 teaspoon water (optional), soy sauce, chili oil

Put the mushrooms in a small bowl with hot water to cover. Let stand 30 to 45 minutes to soften. Cut off and discard the hard stems. Rinse the caps, squeeze them dry, and cut into 1/4-inch-thick slices.

Put the pork, shrimp, water chestnuts, black mushrooms, bamboo shoots, sugar, salt, pepper, and sesame oil in a food processor and chop coarsely (or chop the ingredients finely with a Chinese cleaver).

Place a wok or skillet over high heat and heat the oil. Add the pork mixture and stir-fry 4 to 5 minutes, breaking up the mixture with a spatula. Stir in the cornstarch mixture and cook 1 minute longer, until the liquid has thickened. Set the filling aside and let cool.

Oil two or three 9-inch round cake pans. Set a rack in a pot and add water to a depth of 1 1/2 to 2 inches. (If you are using a steamer, fill the lower tier of the steamer with water.)

Put the wheat starch in a bowl. Bring 1½ cups of water to a boil, then pour it over the wheat starch, stirring with chopsticks or a fork until the dough becomes too thick to stir. Allow the dough to cool just long enough to handle, then knead it with your hands in the bowl. (Be careful handling the hot dough, but don't wait too long—you will get a better result if the dough doesn't cool too much before you knead it.)

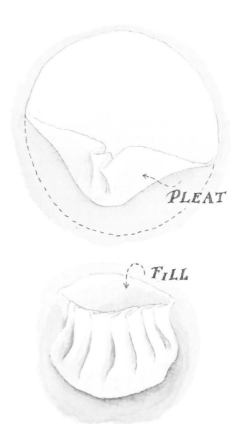

Turn the dough out onto a board lightly dusted with wheat starch. Knead 1 minute, until the wheat starch is well incorporated. (Overkneading will make the dough too chewy, while underkneading will make a dough more prone to cracking or splitting open while cooking.)

Divide the dough into quarters and shape each into a 1½-inch diameter roll. Keep the unused portion in a bowl or on the board, covered with a damp cloth.

Cut the first roll into 7 equal segments. Form one segment into a ball. Roll out into a circle about 3½ inches in diameter. (If you want your *ha gow* to be uniform, use a 3½-inch-diameter cookie cutter, open-ended can, or drinking glass. A 6-ounce tuna can works well. Scraps may be kneaded together and rerolled.)

Pinch 6 or 7 pleats around half the circumference of the circle, creating a pocket. The pleated side should resemble the toe of a baby slipper. Spoon a heaping teaspoon of filling into the pocket, being careful to keep it from touching the edge of the dough. Firmly pinch the pleated side to the unpleated side to seal in the filling. Place the finished *ha gow* in the oiled pans ¾ to 1 inch apart. (They will expand when they cook, so don't try to fit more than 8 to a pan.)

Bring the water in the pot or steamer to a boil. Lower a pan onto the rack (or upper tiers of the steamer), cover, and steam 8 minutes over high heat. The dough will look raw and white when you open the pot but will become translucent as soon as it cools a little. Keep warm while you cook the remaining batches, adding water to the pan as needed. Serve hot, with small dishes of condiments for dipping.

Siu Mai

These are perhaps the easiest dim sum to make, since there are no compli-cated folds to learn, nor do you have to worry about seams splitting open during cooking. If you have a few extra minutes, chop the filling by hand instead of using a food processor; one aunt insists that the results are far superior. A bamboo steamer is the best way to cook the dumplings, but a large pot and round cake pans work just fine.

3–4	dried black mushrooms
1	pound pork shoulder or boneless country-style spareribs (not too lean), cut into 1-inch cubes
12	ounces shrimp, peeled and deveined
2	green onions, cut into ½-inch lengths
4	ounces bamboo shoots, sliced
2	teaspoons soy sauce
2	teaspoons salt
1¼	teaspoons sugar
1	teaspoon cornstarch
¼	teaspoon sesame oil
⅛	teaspoon white pepper
1	egg
1	16-ounce package siu mai wrappers (see Note)
2	tablespoons fresh or frozen green peas
¼	carrot, cut into ¼-inch dice

CONDIMENTS
1   teaspoon Coleman's Hot Mustard mixed with 1 teaspoon water (optional, soy sauce, hot chili oil, sesame oil

Put the mushrooms in a small bowl with hot water to cover. Let stand 30 to 45 minutes to soften. Cut off and discard the hard stems. Rinse the caps, squeeze them dry, and cut into ¼-inch-thick slices.

Combine the mushrooms, pork, shrimp, green onions, bamboo shoots, soy sauce, salt, sugar, cornstarch, sesame oil, white pepper, and egg in a food proces-sor and pulse several times until the ingredients are coarsely ground. (If you choose to chop the mixture with a cleaver, use your hands to mix in the egg halfway through chopping.)

Oil three 8- or 9-inch round pans or the upper tiers of a steamer. Set a rack in a pot and add water to a depth of 1½ to 2 inches. (If you are using a steamer, fill the lower tier two-thirds full with water and oil the upper tiers.)

Place a *siu mai* wrapper on a clean work surface, spoon a heaping tablespoon of filling into the center, and gather the edges up the sides, forming a cup. Flatten the bottom of the *siu mai* on your work surface; the filling will remain exposed at the top. Press a pea and carrot cube into the filling. Arrange the finished *siu mai* at least ½ inch apart in the pans or steamer tiers.

Bring the water in the pot or steamer to a boil. Lower a pan onto the rack (or stack the steamer tiers together) and steam over high heat for 15 minutes. Put the finished *siu mai* on a serving platter, cover them loosely with foil, and keep warm while you steam the next batches. Replenish the pot with water as necessary between batches.

Serve hot, with small dishes of condiments for dipping.

NOTE: Also known as *sue gow* wrappers or dumpling skins, available at Asian markets or in the freezer section at some supermarkets. (Each package contains 60 to 70 wrappers. The unused portion may be wrapped well and refrozen.) You may substitute wonton wrappers, which are more widely available, but they will have a slightly different texture when cooked. Do not substitute potsticker wrappers, which are too thick and heavy.

Baked Char Siu Bao

A shiny egg glaze helps these brown nicely. You may use cooked *char siu* from an Asian take-out delicatessen, or make your own (page 137) for the filling. If you are making the filling 1 day ahead, allow it to reach room temperature before stuffing and baking the *bao*.

DOUGH

6–7 cups all-purpose flour

1 teaspoon salt

½ cup sugar

½ cup vegetable shortening

¼ cup lukewarm water

1 tablespoon dry yeast

2 cups milk

1 cup water

 Vegetable or peanut oil

FILLING

3 tablespoons sugar

3 tablespoons oyster sauce

1 teaspoon soy sauce

½ teaspoon sesame oil

3 tablespoons hoisin sauce

1 tablespoon dry sherry or rice wine

1 tablespoon vegetable or peanut oil

1 garlic clove, finely chopped

2 tablespoons finely chopped yellow onion

1¼ pounds Classic Char Siu (page 137), cut into ½-inch dice

1 tablespoon cornstarch mixed with 2 tablespoons water

1 egg, lightly beaten

In a large bowl, mix together 5 cups of the flour, the salt, and sugar with a wire whisk. With a pastry blender or 2 knives, cut in the shortening until the flour resembles coarse meal.

In a small bowl, combine the lukewarm water with the yeast and let it soften 5 minutes.

Combine the milk and ¾ cup of the water in a medium saucepan and heat to 110°F. to 115°F. Remove from the heat and stir in the yeast mixture. Add this to the flour mixture and mix well.

Add another 1 cup of flour and mix until the dough becomes a sticky, some-what shaggy mass. Turn the dough out onto a well-floured board and knead 5 to 8 minutes, until the dough is smooth and elastic, adding flour to the board as necessary to keep the dough from sticking.

Generously oil a clean large bowl. Place the dough in the bowl and turn to coat all sides. Cover the bowl with plastic wrap and let the dough rise in a warm, draft-free place for 2½ hours, until doubled in bulk.

Oil 2 cookie sheets and set aside.

While the dough is rising, make the filling. In a bowl, mix the sugar, oyster sauce, soy sauce, sesame oil, hoisin sauce, and dry sherry. Set aside.

Place a wok or large skillet over medium-high heat and heat the oil. Add the garlic and onion and stir-fry for 1 minute. Stir in the *char siu* and sauce mixture and mix to coat the meat well. Stir in the cornstarch mixture, lower the heat, and cook 1 to 2 minutes longer, until the sauce has thickened. Allow to cool thoroughly. The filling can be made 1 day ahead; allow it to reach room temperature before filling the *bao.*

Punch down the risen dough and turn it out onto a floured board. Pat the dough into an 8 × 12-inch rectangle, then cut it into 24 equal portions, each about 2 inches square.

Put a portion of dough in one palm and flatten it with your fingers into a 3-inch circle slightly thicker in the middle than around the edges. Place a heaping tablespoon of filling in the center. Pinch the dough together firmly to seal in the filling completely.

Put the *bao,* pinched side down, on the prepared cookie sheet. Continue with the remaining dough and filling, placing the finished *bao* 2 inches apart on the cookie sheets so that they will have room to expand. Cover the *bao* loosely with plastic wrap and let rise in a warm, draft-free place for 30 minutes.

Preheat the oven to 350°F.

With a pastry brush, brush the *bao* lightly with the beaten egg. Bake the *bao* for 15 to 20 minutes, or until golden brown. To test for doneness, take out 1 *bao* and tear it in half; the bread should be airy rather than raw-looking and doughy.

Transfer the *bao* to a wire rack and cool slightly before serving.

NOTE: The baked *bao* may be refrigerated for a day or frozen. Allow the *bao* to reach room temperature, then reheat 5 or 6 minutes in a 350°F. oven.

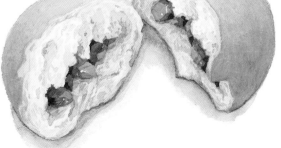

Baked Sweet Bao

MAKES 24 BAO

These can be served for breakfast, as part of a Chinese buffet lunch, or as a sweet final treat for a dim sum meal. Make the filling 1 day ahead.

1 recipe Lotus Seed Paste (page 66), chilled, or Sweet Black Bean Paste variation (page 67)

Vegetable or peanut oil
1 recipe bao dough (page 62)
Few drops of red food coloring

If using lotus seed paste, remove it from the refrigerator. While it is still cold, measure rounded tablespoonfuls into 24 equal portions, shaping each portion into a ball. Space them apart on a plate and allow them to reach room temperature. If using the bean paste, allow it to reach room temperature. You do not need to shape it.

Oil 2 cookie sheets and set aside.

Prepare the dough as for Baked *Char Siu Bao* (page 62) and set it aside to rise for 2½ hours. After the dough has risen, punch it down. Turn it out onto a floured board and pat it into an 8 × 12-inch rectangle. Cut it into 24 equal portions, each about 2 inches square.

Put a portion of the dough in one palm and flatten it with your fingers into a 3-inch circle slightly thicker in the center than around the edges. Place a portion of lotus seed paste or a rounded tablespoon of bean paste in the center and pinch the dough together firmly to seal in the paste completely.

Put the *bao* pinched side down on the oiled cookie sheet. Continue with the remaining dough and filling, placing the finished *bao* 2 inches apart on the prepared cookie sheets so that they will have room to expand. Cover the *bao* loosely with plastic wrap and let rise in a warm, draft-free place for 30 minutes.

Preheat the oven to 350°F.

With a pastry brush, brush the *bao* lightly with the beaten egg. Put a few drops of food coloring onto a small dish. Dip the end of a

MARK SWEET BAO WITH A STRAW DIPPED INTO RED FOOD COLOR

drinking straw or a chopstick into the food coloring, then press it lightly onto the center of the *bao*. Bake the *bao* for 15 to 20 minutes, or until golden brown. To check for doneness, take out 1 *bao* and tear it in half; the bread should be airy rather than raw-looking and doughy.

Transfer the *bao* to wire racks and cool slightly before serving.

NOTE: The baked *bao* may be refrigerated for a day or frozen. Allow the *bao* to reach room temperature, then reheat 5 or 6 minutes in a 350° F. oven.

Manners

ELLEN

Self-promotion is a very American trait, but to the Chinese, it's considered bad form to say anything good about oneself. "No, my food is terrible. Yours is the best!" "Your child is the smartest. Mine never studies." "No, thank you, don't go to any trouble. We just ate." We were taught to deny every compliment, push every gift back with vehement protests, automatically say no to every offer of food. It took years for us to learn the phrase, "Yes, please," because it seemed so shockingly forward and blunt.

It would not be wise to take these statements literally. The "terrible" food was probably carefully planned and painstakingly cooked. The child who "never studies" was likely the brightest, most studious one in his or her class. Worst of all, not pushing food and drink on a guest, whether or not he or she "just ate," was considered exceedingly inhospitable.

One is never to cook just enough to feed everyone; the table must still be heavily laden when everyone is finished. No one arrives for a visit without shopping bags full of fruit, meats, and cookies. No one returns home without the equivalent amount of food—or more.

More than once, as a car full of unexpected guests rolled into the driveway, my mother has sneaked out the back door and raced to town to buy groceries for an elaborate lunch. The guests would protest endlessly afterward that they were unworthy of so much fuss. Never mind that, arriving just before noon, they knew any self-respecting hostess would provide lunch.

Little is communicated directly. It is understood that one just knows how to conduct oneself honorably. When in doubt, exceed.

Lotus Seed Paste

MAKES ABOUT 2 CUPS

Cooking with dried lotus seeds used to require soaking the seeds before tediously scraping off their very thin skins. Now that the seeds are available already skinned, this is a simple recipe. The paste may be used to fill *Lek Doi* (page 68) or Baked Sweet *Bao* (page 64); it freezes well. Unlike canned lotus seed paste, which is dark and oily, homemade lotus seed paste has a delicate flavor.

6 *ounces lotus seeds (about 1⅓ cups dried)*

1½ *cups sugar*

3 *tablespoons vegetable oil*

Rinse the lotus seeds in a colander. Put in a large bowl, cover with about 5 cups of water, and soak for 2 hours or overnight. Drain well.

Open the seeds and remove the bitter green buds inside, then place the seeds in a heavy saucepan with 3 cups of water and bring to a boil. Lower the heat and simmer, covered, until tender, about 2½ to 3 hours. You may need to add a little water toward the end of the cooking time to keep the seeds from burning. They will be very soft. Mash the seeds with a potato masher or puree them in a food processor or blender and return the puree to the saucepan.

Stir in the sugar and oil and cook, uncovered, over medium-low heat for 30 to 35 minutes, stirring frequently. Lower the heat if the paste begins to burn. The paste should become slightly translucent and quite thick; it will become firmer as it cools.

Put the lotus seed paste in a bowl, cover, and refrigerate for up to 3 days.

Sweet Red Bean Paste

MAKES 2 CUPS

You can make a smoother paste by putting the ingredients in the food processor. However, Ellen's mother remarked that our hand-mashed bean paste had the exact texture of her grandmother's in China. The beans require overnight soaking. Bean paste can be used as a filling for *Lek Doi* (page 68), and Baked Sweet *Bao* (page 64). It freezes well.

1 cup dried adzuki beans

3 tablespoons vegetable oil

½ cup packed brown sugar

Wash the adzuki beans and place in a saucepan with enough water to cover plus 2 cups. Soak overnight at room temperature.

Drain the beans, then return to the pan with 2½ cups fresh water. Bring the beans to a boil, lower the heat to a simmer, and cook, covered, for about 1 hour, or until the beans are tender. Puree the beans with their cooking liquid in a food processor or mash them with a potato masher.

Return the beans to the saucepan. Add the oil and brown sugar and continue to simmer, covered, for 45 minutes to 1 hour, stirring frequently to prevent sticking and burning. The bean paste should become quite thick; it will thicken more after it cools.

VARIATIONS

◆ **With Black Beans:** Substitute black beans for the adzuki beans for a filling called *dow sah*.

◆ **With White Beans:** Substitute white beans for the adzuki beans and use it in place of Lotus Seed Paste, opposite. It will have a different texture.

Lek Doi (Chinese Doughnuts)

MAKES ABOUT 24 *LEK DOI*

A well-made lek doi has thin, even walls

Lek doi are made to celebrate birthdays and Chinese New Year. These are not the heavy, thick-walled fried dough balls that appear on many dim sum carts. A cook's reputation can rest on her ability to create an airy ball with thin, even walls and a chewy texture, enclosing the merest hint of filling. In our family, one relative is held in high esteem for being able to cook eight of these at a time, keeping track of each like a skilled juggler as she rolls and presses them in a wok full of hot oil.

Lek doi can be sweet or savory, depending on your choice of filling. They are best if served within an hour of cooking.

DOUGH
- 1   *pound glutinous rice flour*
- 1   *cup sugar*
- 1½   *cups water, approximately*
- ⅔   *cup mashed cooked or canned yams*
- ½   *cup sesame seeds*
- 7–8   *cups peanut oil for deep-frying*

FILLINGS (choose one or more)
Sweet Red Bean Paste (page 67); Lotus Seed Paste (page 66); ½ cup coconut mixed with ¼ cup chopped peanuts; Savory Chinese Sausage Filling (page 70)

In a large bowl, stir together the rice flour, sugar, ¾ cup of the water, and the mashed yams. Add the remaining water a little at a time as needed to moisten the flour. When the dough becomes too dense to stir, mix it with your hands, kneading it vigorously in the bowl for at least 3 minutes to develop the gluten. The dough should be fairly stiff but not dry; add more water or rice flour if needed. Divide the dough into 24 equal portions, each about the size of a large apricot. Place them in a clean bowl and cover with a damp cloth or plastic wrap to keep the dough from drying out as you work.

Roll one portion of dough into a ball. Make an indentation in it with a thumb, then form the dough into a bowl shape about ¼ inch thick. Scoop a rounded teaspoon of filling into the center. (If you use too much filling, it is likely to leak into the cooking oil. Black specks of burned filling will stick to other *lek doi* as you cook them, and you will have to scoop out what you can with a fine mesh sieve.) Gather up the edges and pinch them together to seal in the filling completely. Roll the dough between your palms to form a smooth ball.

Place about 1 tablespoon of the sesame seeds in a shallow dish. Roll the ball in the seeds, then roll it between your palms again to embed the seeds in the dough. Set the finished balls aside on a cookie sheet. Repeat with the remaining dough, replenishing the dish as needed with about a tablespoon of sesame seeds at a time.

Line 2 cookie sheets with several layers of paper towels and set aside.

Pour enough oil into the wok to come within about 2½ inches from the top of a heavy Dutch oven or wok. A wok with a flat bottom and long handle works best because you will be pressing against the sides and you must keep the wok very steady when it is full of hot oil. Heat the oil to 380°F.

Carefully lower 2 or 3 *lek doi* into the oil one at a time. (You may want to try cooking the first one by itself.) Cook, rotating them gently but constantly with the mesh strainer, for 1 minute.

As the balls begin to float to the surface, begin to press them against the sides of the pan with the back of the wire mesh strainer, rotating and pressing them continually and with increasing pressure as they begin to puff up. This stretches the dough evenly all around, creating a lighter, rounder result. (Be careful not to press too hard at first or the filling may leak out.)

Cook until browned and puffed like balloons, pressing against the sides all the while, for about 5 minutes, keeping the heat between 375°F. and 380°F. Drain the finished *lek doi* on the prepared cookie sheet and serve as soon as possible. *Lek doi* will keep their light texture for only a few hours. Leftover *lek doi* are usually reheated by steaming for 5 or 10 minutes over high heat. They will become soft and sticky.

Savory Chinese Sausage Filling

This filling provides a pleasant savory contrast to the slightly sweet *Lek Doi* (page 68). It can be made a day or two in advance.

4–6   *dried cloud ears*

2   *Chinese sausages, cut into ¼-inch dice*

2   *tablespoons preserved daikon radish, finely chopped (optional) (see Note)*

¼   *cup minced cilantro leaves (optional)*

1   *green onion, thinly sliced*

    Pinch of sugar

Put the cloud ears in a bowl and cover them with hot water. Let stand 30 minutes to soften. Rinse and squeeze them dry. Cut off and discard any hard parts, then mince the cloud ears finely.

Heat a nonstick skillet over medium-high heat. Add the diced sausages and stir-fry for 30 seconds. Add the remaining ingredients and stir-fry 30 seconds longer. Set aside to cool or refrigerate in a covered container for up to 2 days.

NOTE: Preserved daikon radish is essential for the flavor that we remember. However, the filling is still quite tasty without them.

GARDEN FRESH: VEGETABLES

We used to have vegetable gardens with ample produce to harvest almost daily and share with relatives. However they were cooked, vegetables were always enhanced with seasoning. In some of these recipes the vegetables are pickled, or lightly cooked and simply dressed. More often, they are stir-fried with meat, chicken, or seafood, which add their own flavor, texture, and body. Those dishes can serve either as a colorful course in a Chinese meal or as a stand-alone meal when served over steamed rice.

ONE IS ALWAYS TO CHOOSE THE VERY BEST TO GIVE AWAY.

Pickled Carrots and Daikon Radish

MAKES ABOUT 2 CUPS

This is a traditional side dish at a new baby celebration, but it is also a refreshing side dish for a meal with heavy, rich flavors. You may reduce the quantity of ginger or omit it entirely if it is too hot for your taste. If you can find it, young ginger has a milder flavor and less fibrous texture. You may also use either all carrots or all radish. Prepare 2 days ahead for the best flavor.

½   cup water

½   cup cider vinegar

1   cup sugar

2   carrots

1   medium daikon radish, about 1 pound

1   4-inch piece ginger (optional)

2   tablespoons salt

2   teaspoons sesame seeds

Combine the water, vinegar, and sugar in a small enamel saucepan and bring to a boil over medium heat, stirring occasionally, until the sugar has dissolved, about 4 minutes. Remove from the heat and cool to room temperature.

Peel the carrots, cutting off and discarding both ends. Cut the carrots diagonally into paper-thin slices. You may want to use a vegetable peeler.

Peel the radish, cutting off and discarding both ends. Cut the radish crosswise at 1¼-inch intervals. Placing the cut side down, cut lengthwise into paper-thin slices. Again, you may want to use a vegetable peeler. If the slices are very wide, cut them in half lengthwise.

If using, peel, then cut the ginger diagonally into paper-thin slices.

Place the carrots, radish, and ginger in a shallow bowl and sprinkle with the salt. Let stand 20 minutes. Place in a colander and rinse well under cold water. Squeeze dry and place in a clean quart jar. Pour the brine over and stir lightly to distribute evenly. Cover and refrigerate for 2 days before serving.

Place a nonstick skillet over medium heat. Add the sesame seeds and toast until they are lightly browned, about 2 minutes, shaking the pan gently. Remove the sesame seeds immediately to cool. (Leaving them in the hot skillet may cause them to burn.)

Remove the carrots, radish, and ginger from the jar with a slotted spoon or chopsticks. Serve in small shallow dishes, sprinkled with toasted sesame seeds.

Asparagus with Soy Dressing

MAKES 3 TO 4 SERVINGS

Our family used to exchange produce with other farmers. It was a good way to vary the monotony of a diet based on one's own abundant but limited crop. We used to receive big boxes of asparagus every summer and this was a favorite way to serve it.

1 *pound asparagus, medium spears*

2 *teaspoons soy sauce*

2 *teaspoons vegetable or peanut oil*

Few drops of sesame oil (optional)

Wash the asparagus carefully to remove all traces of sand. Snap off the tough ends and cut into 3- to 4-inch pieces if very long.

Put 6 cups water in a medium saucepan and bring to a rolling boil. Add the asparagus and cook about 2 minutes, or until it is beginning to get soft but is still bright green.

Drain the asparagus, return it to the empty pot, and toss it with the soy sauce, oil, and sesame oil, if using. Serve hot or at room temperature.

Sesame Spinach

This works well as a side dish on its own, but it's prettiest when spread around the edge of a platter to set off a dish with contrasting colors, such as Squid Tossed with Soy Sauce and Oil (page 96) or Pan-Fried Prawns in Ketchup Sauce (page 88).

1   *pound fresh spinach leaves (about 2 bunches)*

1   *cup water*

1   *green onion (white part and 3 inches of the green), thinly sliced*

1   *garlic clove, minced*

Dash of black pepper

2   *teaspoons soy sauce*

1   *teaspoon sesame oil*

2   *teaspoons sesame seeds*

Cut off and discard the stems from the spinach; wash thoroughly and drain.

In a large, nonaluminum (preferably enamel) saucepan, bring the water to a boil. Add the spinach and cook over medium heat until the spinach is just wilted but still bright green, about 2 minutes.

Drain the spinach in a colander, but do not rinse it. Let it cool 5 minutes, then gently press out any excess water, forming a log shape. Chop the log into 5 or 6 segments.

Mix the green onion, garlic, black pepper, soy sauce, and sesame oil in a mixing bowl. Add the spinach and toss gently.

Spread the spinach on a plate (or around the edge of a platter, if you are using it to accompany another dish).

Place a nonstick skillet over medium heat. Add the sesame seeds and toast until they are lightly browned, about 2 minutes, shaking the pan gently. Remove the sesame seeds immediately to cool. (Leaving them in the hot skillet may cause them to burn.) Sprinkle the sesame seeds over the spinach and serve.

chinese Broccoli Tossed with Oyster Sauce and Oils

MAKES 4 TO 6 SERVINGS AS PART
OF A CHINESE MEAL

Gai lan, a flavorful cousin of supermarket broccoli, has narrow, round stalks and leafy tops with small, loose heads of white flowers. It is prized for its bright green color, crisp texture, and almost bitter tang. We had it far less often than the more common, easy-to-grow greens such as bok choy. It is available at Asian grocery stores and sometimes at the supermarket.

1   pound gai lan (*Chinese broccoli*) or regular broccoli

¼   teaspoon salt

½   teaspoon vegetable or peanut oil

½   teaspoon sesame oil

1   tablespoon oyster sauce

Wash the *gai lan*. Cut the ends off the stalks. With a paring knife or vegetable peeler, peel the lower half of the stalks. Halve the *gai lan* crosswise if it is very long. (If using regular broccoli, peel, then cut lengthwise into quarters.)

Add the salt to 3 quarts of water in a large pot and bring to a rapid boil over high heat. Add the *gai lan* and cook over high heat about 7 minutes, stirring occasionally until crisp-tender and still bright green. Test it for doneness by removing a stalk, running it under cold water, cutting off a piece, and biting through it.

Drain the *gai lan*. Toss it to shake off excess water. (You can prepare the *gai lan* to this point up to 3 hours in advance if you want to serve it at room temperature, but do not dress it until just before serving.) Return the *gai lan* to the empty pot and toss gently with the oil, sesame oil, and oyster sauce. Arrange the *gai lan* neatly on a serving platter.

Black Mushrooms in Oyster Sauce

Because the finest mushrooms are so expensive, they are usually used sparingly, as an accent. An entire dish of these was considered a banquet treat, not an everyday dish. Dried black mushrooms are graded and priced by the appearance of their caps, with those that show a deeply ridged starlike pattern most highly prized. They are thicker and have an almost meaty texture when cooked; less expensive ones have a chewier texture, but all grades are intensely flavorful. This tastes best when made a day in advance.

¼ pound dried black mushrooms	Salt
3 cups Simple Chicken Broth (page 19) or canned low-sodium chicken broth	1 head iceberg lettuce (optional) (see Note)
1 ½-inch chunk rock sugar or ½ teaspoon sugar	1 tablespoon vegetable or peanut oil (optional)
5 teaspoons oyster sauce	1 tablespoon cornstarch mixed with ¼ cup cold water or unsalted chicken broth
½ teaspoon soy sauce	

Put the mushrooms in a large bowl and cover with hot water. Let stand 30 to 45 minutes to soften. Cut off and discard the hard stems. Rinse the caps and squeeze them dry.

Put the mushrooms in a large saucepan with the chicken broth. Bring to a boil, lower the heat, and simmer, covered, until the mushrooms are tender, about 1½ hours. Add the sugar and simmer 3 to 4 minutes longer, until the sugar has dissolved. Add the oyster sauce, soy sauce, and salt to taste. (You can prepare the recipe to this point a day ahead and refrigerate.)

Separate the leaves of the iceberg lettuce, if using, and wash them. Fill a large pot two-thirds full with water, add 1 teaspoon salt, and bring to a boil. Drop the lettuce leaves in the water and cook 30 seconds, or until the leaves are just wilted. Drain the leaves and toss them with the oil. Arrange them on a deep serving platter.

FRESH MUSHROOMS *are mildest*

LOWER GRADE *is a bit* *tougher*

BEST GRADE *has a* *crisper bite*

Stir the cornstarch mixture into the mushrooms. Continue cooking until the sauce has thickened. Spoon the mushrooms onto the lettuce-lined platter and serve hot.

NOTE: The lettuce adds a pale green, slightly crunchy contrast to the mushrooms' smooth texture, rich color, and intense flavor. However, you can serve the mushrooms without the lettuce, perhaps garnishing the dish with a few sprigs of cilantro.

VARIATION

Black Mushrooms with Abalone: This dish was occasionally made even more special by the addition of a 15-ounce can of abalone. Cut into ¼-inch slices and stir into the mushrooms during the last minute of cooking just to heat through.

Bitter Melons or Bell Peppers with Chicken in Black Bean Sauce

MAKES 6 TO 8 SERVINGS AS PART OF A CHINESE MEAL

A little sugar balances the cool bitter tang of the bitter melons without making the dish sweet. Nothing can substitute for bitter melon's unique flavor, but you can create a delicious stir-fry variation with bell peppers and yellow onion.

MARINADE

2 teaspoons soy sauce

1 teaspoon dry sherry or rice wine

¼ teaspoon sugar

¾–1 pound skinless boneless, chicken breast, cut into 1-inch pieces

1 pound bitter melons (about 2 medium)

SAUCE

2 tablespoons fermented black beans

1 garlic clove, peeled and crushed

1 tablespoon soy sauce

1 teaspoon dry sherry or rice wine

1¼ teaspoons sugar

½ cup chicken broth

¼ cup chicken broth mixed with 1 tablespoon cornstarch

2 tablespoons vegetable or peanut oil

Mix the marinade ingredients together in a medium bowl. Add the chicken, toss well, and marinate for 20 to 30 minutes.

Meanwhile, cut the stem end off the bitter melons, then halve them lengthwise. Remove the seeds. Cut the bitter melons diagonally into ½-inch slices. Fill a large saucepan two-thirds full with water and bring to a boil. Add the bitter melon slices and cook, uncovered, 3 minutes. Drain, rinse under cold water, and drain again. (This step will reduce the bitterness of the bitter melons and make them cook faster when stir-fried.)

In a small bowl, rinse and drain the black beans, then add the garlic, soy sauce, dry sherry, sugar, and ½ cup chicken broth.

Heat a wok over medium-high heat. Heat 1 tablespoon oil, then add the bitter melon slices and stir-fry until they are almost tender, about 3 to 4 minutes. Remove the bitter melon to a serving dish and keep warm.

Add another tablespoon of oil to the wok, then add the chicken and stir-fry until it is browned and just cooked through, about 4 minutes. Return the bitter melon slices to the wok with the sauce mixture and bring to a boil. Add the cornstarch mixture and continue to cook until the sauce has thickened.

BITTER MELON

VARIATION

With Bell Peppers: Substitute 2 medium green bell peppers, seeded and cut into 1-inch squares, and 1 medium yellow onion, quartered and separated into layers, for the bitter melons. Omit the sugar in the sauce. Stir-fry the peppers and onions 4 to 5 minutes.

Preserving Traditions

ELLEN

In addition to our farm crops, my family planted a large garden and orchard. Chinese vegetables were not available at the local market, so we grew our own long beans, bitter melons, gourds, winter melons, and greens. We also grew corn, squash, peppers, and cucumbers. Summer mornings we were roused at dawn to work in the garden until it became too scorchingly hot to continue. Our reward came at dusk, when we harvested laundry baskets full of succulent sweet corn and boiled them immediately for dessert.

We planted the orchard with peaches, apples, grapes, plums, nectarines, apricots, pomegranates, and Chinese red dates. Mature figs, almonds, and walnuts already grew around the house.

Summers we canned. My face fell when relatives brought over crates brimming with Bartlett pears. I peeled pear after pear next to an air conditioner that feebly countered the steam rising from bubbling kettles full of canning jars.

By summer's end we had also made pickles in sweet vinegar and canned hundreds of jars of peaches, tomatoes, and apricots.

We also preserved produce by drying it. Chinese greens, black figs, bitter melons, and bright red jujube fruit were spread out each morning on aluminum trays and covered with old window screens to dry under the summer sun.

The largest and best vegetables were allowed to go to seed. The seeds were painstakingly extracted, dried, and saved for planting the following year. Seeds for Chinese vegetables not available at local nurseries were exchanged among families and considered cherished gifts.

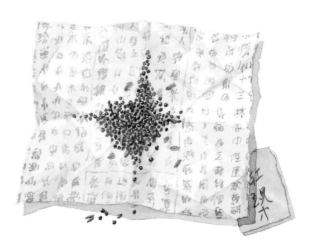

Fried Green Tomatoes with Flank Steak

MAKES 4 TO 6 SERVINGS AS PART OF A CHINESE MEAL

We looked forward to this dish every summer when we couldn't wait for the first tomatoes to ripen. This can also be served over noodles, as a piquant variation of Tomato Beef Chow Mein (page 50).

½ pound flank steak

MARINADE
1 tablespoon cornstarch
1½ teaspoons soy sauce
⅛ teaspoon sugar
1 tablespoon dry sherry or rice wine

1 pound green tomatoes
2 teaspoons soy sauce
⅓ cup cider vinegar
⅓ cup sugar
Vegetable or peanut oil
2½ teaspoons cornstarch mixed with ¼ cup cold water or chicken broth

Cut the flank steak diagonally across the grain into ⅛ × 3 × 1½-inch strips. (This is easier if you freeze the meat about 30 minutes, until firm but not frozen hard, just before cutting it.) Mix the marinade ingredients in a medium bowl, add the flank steak, and marinate 30 minutes.

Cut the tomatoes into ¼-inch-thick slices. Cut the slices into half circles, or quarter circles if they are very large.

Mix the soy sauce, vinegar, and sugar in a small bowl and set aside.

Place a wok over medium-high heat. Heat 1 tablespoon oil, then add the flank steak and stir-fry until it is cooked through, about 3 minutes. Transfer to a platter and keep warm.

Add about 2 teaspoons more oil to the wok if necessary. Add the tomatoes and soy sauce mixture and cook until the tomatoes are tender, about 4 to 6 minutes, stirring occasionally. Add more sugar if the tomatoes are very tart.

Stir in the cornstarch mixture and continue to cook until the sauce has thickened and no longer looks milky.

Add the flank steak and stir-fry until heated through.

Green Loofah Squash with Prawns

Loofah or Silk Squash

It's hard to believe that the rough, exfoliating fibers of the loofah sponge we use in the shower can in its smaller, immature form be more tender than zucchini. In fact, it's aptly described by its other name, silk squash. We used to grow the squash to eat, saving the largest ones for seed. When the squash used for seed turned brown and dry, we sawed them open with a knife to shake out the seeds. We soaked the hulls of the large squash to soften the skins, which then had to be tediously scraped off. The hulls were used to scrub dishes and scour the tub. With occasional bleaching, they lasted for years.

Green loofah squash is available at some Asian markets; you can substitute zucchini, but it has a denser texture and somewhat different flavor.

1 ½ teaspoon chopped fresh ginger

2 teaspoons soy sauce

⅛ teaspoon sugar

1 teaspoon dry sherry or rice wine

1 pound prawns, peeled and deveined

1 pound loofah squash (about 3 medium) or zucchini

1 tablespoon vegetable or peanut oil

4 fresh water chestnuts, peeled and sliced

4 ounces sliced bamboo shoots, rinsed and drained

1 tablespoon oyster sauce

White pepper

1 tablespoon cornstarch mixed with ⅓ cup chicken broth

⅓ cup roasted cashews (optional)

In a medium bowl, combine the ginger, soy sauce, sugar, and dry sherry. Add the prawns and marinate for 30 minutes to 1 hour.

Peel the squash and cut off the ends. Cut diagonally into ¼-inch slices.

Place a wok over high heat. Heat the oil, then add the prawns and stir-fry until they are opaque and bright orange, about 5 minutes. Remove them from the wok and keep warm.

Add the squash and stir-fry until soft, about 3 minutes for loofah squash, 4 to 5 minutes for zucchini. Add the water chestnuts and bamboo shoots and stir-fry 30 seconds. Add the prawns and toss to reheat through, about 30 seconds, then lower the heat to medium and add the oyster sauce and white pepper to taste. Stir in the cornstarch mixture and cook until the sauce has thickened.

Stir in the cashews, if using, just before serving.

VARIATION

Squash with Scallops and Prawns: Substitute ½ pound scallops for half of the prawns. Halve or quarter them if they are very large and marinate and cook them together with the prawns.

Long Beans with Ground Pork in Lettuce Packets

MAKES 4 TO 6 SERVINGS

Here a savory, piping hot filling is wrapped in cool, crunchy lettuce leaves dabbed with sweet hoisin sauce, creating a pleasing combination of flavors and textures.

- 1 head iceberg lettuce (or other crunchy lettuce, such as romaine)
- 1 pound pork shoulder or boneless country-style spareribs (not too lean), cubed
- 1 teaspoon cornstarch
- ⅛ teaspoon sugar
- 2 teaspoons thin soy sauce

- 1 tablespoon dry sherry or rice wine
- ½ pound Chinese long beans or other green beans, cut into ¼-inch pieces
- 1 tablespoon vegetable or peanut oil
- 8–10 fresh or canned water chestnuts, peeled if fresh, and finely chopped
- 2 tablespoons oyster sauce
- About ⅓ cup hoisin sauce

Separate, wash, and dry the lettuce leaves. Large leaves can be cut in half. Put the leaves on a serving plate and refrigerate, covered.

Place the pork cubes in a food processor and pulse until chopped medium-fine. (If you prefer, you can chop the pork finely with a Chinese cleaver.) Transfer the pork to a medium bowl and mix with the cornstarch, sugar, soy sauce, and dry sherry. Marinate in the refrigerator for 30 minutes and up to 2 hours.

Bring 4 cups of water to a boil in a medium saucepan. Cook the beans for 2 minutes, drain, and set aside.

Place a wok over medium-high heat, then heat the oil. Add the pork and stir-fry, breaking up the pork with a spatula until it loses its pink color, about 7 minutes.

Add the long beans and water chestnuts and stir-fry 2 minutes. Stir in the oyster sauce and cook 30 seconds longer. Put the mixture on a serving plate.

To serve, put the plates of pork, lettuce, and a small bowl of hoisin sauce on the table. Have guests take a lettuce leaf, spread a little hoisin sauce on it, add a few spoonfuls of the pork, and wrap the lettuce around the pork to eat as finger food.

✦ **Long Beans with Dried Oysters:** Soak 3 to 6 dried oysters in enough water to cover for 24 hours. Rinse well to remove any sand. Trim off any tough parts. Mince the oysters finely. Add to the pork with the long beans and water chestnuts and proceed as above. Dried oysters have a strong flavor and are an acquired taste, so you may want to try just a little at first.

✦ **Simple Long Beans with Ground Pork:** Omit the water chestnuts, lettuce wrappers, and hoisin sauce dip. Use 1 pound beans. Add ½ cup chicken broth to the wok with the long beans. Mix 2 teaspoons cornstarch with ¼ cup water or chicken broth and stir into the sauce. Cook until the sauce has thickened and the beans are just tender. You can also add 2 to 3 finely diced hot peppers, such as Anaheim or jalapeño. Serve with rice.

ACTUAL SIZE ~ LONG BEAN

Eggs Foo Yung
with Chinese Chives

Gao choy, Chinese chives, grew well in our gardens. Also called garlic chives, they have flat leaves and a stronger flavor than standard supermarket chives. These simple egg pancakes were one of our favorite ways to use Chinese chives. We do not recommend substituting regular chives, since they have a slightly bitter flavor and not enough texture for this recipe, but you can use thinly sliced green onions, which need not be blanched.

1 bunch gao choy *(Chinese chives)*	Vegetable or peanut oil for frying
3 eggs	2 teaspoons oyster sauce
½ cup cooked baby shrimp *(see Note)*	

Wash the chives, discard the stem ends, and chop the green part into ¼-inch lengths; you should have about 1 cup.

Bring 2 cups of water to a boil in a small saucepan, add the chives, and blanch for 30 seconds. Drain the chives, rinse under cold water, and squeeze dry.

Break the eggs into a medium bowl and whisk with a fork. Mix in the shrimp, if using, and the blanched chives.

Place a nonstick skillet over medium heat. Brush the skillet lightly with oil. Ladle a scant ¼ cup of the egg mixture into the pan for each pancake, making 1 or 2 at a time.

When the pancakes are set around the edges, about 1 minute, turn them over carefully and brown on the other side, about 30 seconds. Transfer the finished pancakes to a warmed platter in a single layer while you cook the remaining egg batter.

Drizzle the oyster sauce evenly over the finished pancakes and serve warm.

NOTE: You may substitute finely diced larger shrimp, *char siu* (pages 136–137), or ham, or omit this altogether.

GAO CHOY ~ Chinese Chives

FISH AND SEAFOOD

Seafood can be prepared simply and subtly or take on complex flavors and textures, depending on the cook's mood and availability of ingredients. The most important thing to remember about cooking with seafood is that you must start with fresh ingredients.

The simplest way to prepare fish is to steam it. Steaming brings out the pure flavor of fish; it stays firm and moist, and a light topping of ginger, scallions, soy sauce, and oil complements the mildly flavored flesh beautifully. However, our family prepared fish in many different ways, always choosing the method that would best showcase the flavors and textures of the particular fish being prepared.

Pan-frying fish and shrimp seals in the juices and browns the seafood at the same time. Stir-frying fish and shellfish such as clams combines the seafood flavor with the other ingredients in the dish. Deep-frying adds texture and flavor to fish, shrimp, and oysters. The piping hot, light crispy coating is a delightful contrast to the delicate seafood.

PAN-FRIED PRAWNS in KETCHUP SAUCE

Pan-Fried Prawns in Ketchup Sauce

As children we were taught how to shell prawns with our teeth. We held onto the prawns with chopsticks but didn't otherwise use our fingers. It was permissible to spit the shells out onto our plates. This practice may seem crude to those who adhere to Western etiquette. Too bad, because prawns have far more flavor when cooked in the shells. You may shell them before cooking if you must, but it's not the same dish at all. The prawns and sauce can be prepared early in the day, then cooked just before serving. (See illustration, page 87.)

1 pound prawns in the shell	½ teaspoon sesame oil
2 tablespoons ketchup	1 tablespoon vegetable or peanut oil
1 tablespoon oyster sauce	2 green onions, cut into 1-inch pieces
⅛ teaspoon white pepper	

With a sharp knife, cut each prawn through the shell just far enough to expose the sand vein down the back. Remove the sand vein. Rinse the prawns and pat them dry. (This step is important, otherwise the prawns will not brown properly.) Cut off the sharp point from the tails, but leave the rest of the shell intact.

In a small bowl, combine the ketchup, oyster sauce, white pepper, and sesame oil and set aside.

cut through shell

cut off point

Place a large skillet or wok over high heat and heat the oil. Place the prawns in the pan in a single layer. Brown on one side, about 3 minutes, then turn them over to brown the other side, about 3 to 4 minutes longer. Lower the heat to medium, add the ketchup mixture, and stir to coat the prawns well. Add the green onions and continue to cook just long enough to bring out the color of the green onions, about 30 seconds. Serve immediately.

Pan-Fried Prawns in the Shell

This is a simple, colorful recipe. Leaving the shells on keeps the prawns hot and juicy. A frame of Sesame Spinach (page 74) around the edge of the platter would contrast nicely with this dish.

1	pound prawns in the shell	1	teaspoon soy sauce
4	teaspoons vegetable or peanut oil	1	tablespoon dry sherry or rice wine
½	teaspoon salt	2	green onions, cut into 1-inch pieces

With a sharp knife, cut each prawn through the shell just far enough to expose the sand vein down the back. Remove the sand vein. Rinse the prawns and pat them dry. (This step is important, otherwise the prawns will not brown properly.) Cut off the sharp point from the tails, but leave the rest of the shell intact. (See illustration, opposite.)

Place a large skillet or wok over high heat and heat the oil. Add the salt and place the prawns in the pan in a single layer. Brown on one side, about 3 minutes, then turn them over to brown the other side, about 3 to 4 minutes longer.

Add the soy sauce, dry sherry, and green onions. Cook about 1 minute longer, tossing to coat the prawns well. Serve immediately.

Batter-Fried Prawns

Marinating the prawns before frying sets these crisp morsels apart from their American-style counterparts. A bed of shredded lettuce provides a refreshing contrasting crunch, and although our families never used lemon juice, a few drops cut the richness of the seafood.

MARINADE

- 1 tablespoon cornstarch
- ¾ teaspoon minced fresh ginger
- 1 teaspoon soy sauce
- 1 teaspoon dry sherry or rice wine
- Pinch of sugar

- 1 pound prawns, peeled and deveined
- 4–6 leaves romaine or iceberg lettuce, finely shredded, for garnish (optional)
- 1 lemon, for garnish (optional)

BATTER

- ½ cup all-purpose flour
- ¼ cup cornstarch
- ¼ teaspoon baking powder
- ½ teaspoon salt
- ½ cup water

About 6 cups peanut oil for deep-frying

In a medium bowl, combine the cornstarch with the ginger, soy sauce, dry sherry, and sugar. Add the prawns and marinate for 30 minutes.

If using, arrange the shredded lettuce evenly on a serving platter; cut the lemon into 6 wedges and arrange them around the edge. Set aside.

In a medium bowl, mix the flour, cornstarch, baking powder, salt, and water with a wire whisk until smooth. The batter should be easy to stir but not runny. If the batter seems too thick, stir in 1 to 2 tablespoons more water.

Fill a wok or deep fryer with oil to within 2½ to 3 inches below the rim. Clip a candy thermometer to the edge of the wok and heat the oil to 375°F. Line a cookie sheet with several layers of paper towels and set aside.

Dip the prawns one at a time into the batter, letting any excess batter drip back into the bowl. One by one, lower the prawns quickly but carefully into the hot oil, cooking them in 3 or 4 batches. With a wire strainer or slotted spoon, move the prawns around so that they brown evenly. Adjust the heat as needed to maintain an oil temperature of 365°F. to 370°F. The prawns should be brown and crisp in 3 to 4 minutes. Drain them on the prepared cookie sheet. Scoop up and discard any stray bits of batter from the oil.

Arrange the prawns on the lettuce-lined platter and serve immediately, as the prawns become soggy quickly.

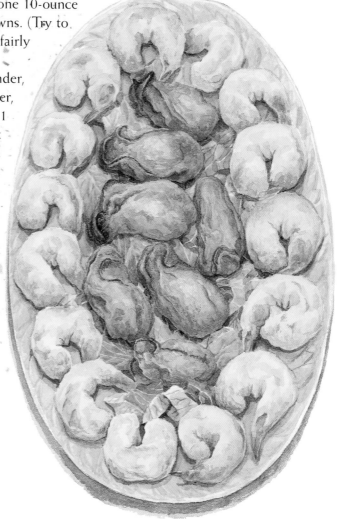

VARIATION

Batter-Fried Oysters: Substitute one 10-ounce jar of shucked oysters for the prawns. (Try to find a jar that contains oysters of fairly uniform size.)

Empty the oysters into a colander, rinse them gently under cold water, and drain. Sprinkle with salt and 1 tablespoon of cornstarch and mix lightly. Bring 4 cups of water to a boil in a small saucepan. Add the oysters and cook over medium heat for 2 to 3 minutes, just until firm. Drain the oysters, rinse them again, and drain. Marinate as for the shrimp, doubling the quantities for the marinade, then dip in batter and fry as above, cooking the oysters in 1 or 2 batches, about 4 minutes each.

Fried Shrimp Balls

These make a wonderful hot appetizer, although we had them most often on a plate with batter-fried oysters at family parties.

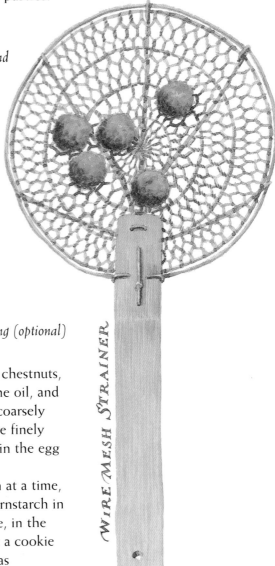

WIRE MESH STRAINER

1½ pounds shrimp, peeled and deveined

4 fresh or canned water chestnuts, peeled if fresh, and quartered

2 green onions, white parts only, cut into ½-inch pieces

2 ounces pork shoulder or country-style spareribs, cut in small cubes (optional)

1 tablespoon egg white

¾ teaspoon salt

¾ teaspoon sugar

¼ teaspoon sesame oil

⅛ teaspoon white pepper

Cornstarch

2 quarts peanut oil for deep-frying

Sweet-and-Sour Sauce (see page 142), for dipping (optional)

In a food processor, combine the shrimp, water chestnuts, green onions, pork, egg white, salt, sugar, sesame oil, and pepper. Pulse several times until the mixture is coarsely ground. (If you prefer, you can chop the mixture finely with a Chinese cleaver. Use your hands to mix in the egg white halfway through chopping.)

Roll the shrimp mixture, a rounded teaspoon at a time, into 1-inch balls. Put about 2 tablespoons of cornstarch in a small dish. Roll the shrimp balls, one at a time, in the cornstarch and set them about ½ inch apart on a cookie sheet or tray. Add more cornstarch to the dish as necessary.

Cover 2 cookie sheets with several layers of paper towels.

In a wok or deep fryer, heat the oil to 370°F. Carefully drop 10 to 12 shrimp balls into the oil, one at a time. Cook 5 to 6 minutes, moving them around gently with a wire strainer or slotted spoon so that they will not stick together, until cooked through and nicely browned. Test for doneness by cutting through a finished ball. The pork should not be pink and the center should not look translucent. Remove the balls with a wire strainer or slotted spoon and drain them on the paper-towel-covered cookie sheets. Cover loosely with foil and keep warm in a 200°F. oven while you continue cooking batches of 10 to 12 balls at a time.

Serve hot. If you are serving this as an appetizer, you may want to spear the balls with toothpicks and serve them with a small bowl of Sweet-and-Sour Sauce for dipping.

San Francisco Banquets

ELLEN

About once a year, we were invited to an elaborate banquet in San Francisco to celebrate a wedding or special birthday. Chinese honor the older passing decades (counting from age one at birth) and mark fifty-first, sixty-first, seventy-first, and eighty-first birthdays with ever larger celebrations.

My siblings and I stared in wonder as my father transformed himself from a dust-covered farmer in khakis and heavy work boots into an elegant stranger in a silver-gray suit and snowy-white shirt, his silk tie secured with a large jade tie-pin.

These were the only times my mother wore one of her Chinese silk *cheong sam*, form-fitting dresses with stiff mandarin collars. One white satin dress was richly embroidered with multicolored metallic threads in the shape of a fantastic dragon. Others depicted intricate butterflies, chrysanthemums, or spring blossoms. Gold and jade jewelry were retrieved from their hiding places, and my mother became a Chinese Cinderella, ready for the ball.

My brothers donned two-toned suits with clip-on bow ties. Tracks through their slicked-back hair betrayed the liberal use of heavily scented Dixie Peach Pomade.

My mother rolled the girls' hair tightly in metal curlers to set overnight. The next morning, barrettes, ribbons, and bobby pins were needed to tame the resulting nest of kinks. My sister and I squirmed in our thin nylon party dresses rich with itchy lace puffed sleeves bulging beneath warm sweaters.

Sometimes our family was too large to sit at a single table, so children might be seated with a table full of strangers speaking a different dialect. Conversation was exhausted once we had dutifully reported our age and grade in school.

Guests of honor were introduced with long speeches, their importance marked by the fanciness of their corsages or boutonnieres. When the couples rising briefly for recognition were wearing carnations instead of orchids, we knew it was almost time to eat.

All at once, bustling waiters paraded in with heavy tureens of steaming birds' nest or shark's fin soup, the first of eight or nine courses, and dinner was under way.

The soup was often followed by crispy-skinned chicken surrounded by colorful shrimp-flavored rice chips. Abalone and black mushrooms were redolent with oyster sauce. Glossy, mahogany-colored Peking duck was served with steamed buns and piquant hoisin sauce. Succulent shrimp and scallops were tossed with bamboo shoots, snow peas, fresh water chestnuts, and enormous cashews. Whole steamed fish lay under blankets of slivered ginger and green onions.

We children should have been more appreciative, but banquets severely tested our limited ability to sit still. Throughout the numbing procession of courses, we grew tired and bored, and would put squab heads on one another's plates or hold surreptitious sword fights with chopsticks held in our laps.

At the end of the meal, the adults always bustled about, eyeing one another's finery, loudly exchanging the latest gossip with seldom-seen relatives, or guffawing with old friends from China days. In a sea of satin and shiny suits, we reluctant children were nudged forward by our parents so relatives could pat our heads and ask if we were studying hard. Finally, with sated palates and much news to reflect upon, we dispersed into the night.

Clams and Mussels in Black Bean Sauce

MAKES 6 TO 8 SERVINGS AS PART OF A CHINESE MEAL

Eat the shellfish over rice so that you catch all the richly flavored juices.

- 1 pound small clams (littleneck, cherrystone, or manila) (see Note)
- 1 pound mussels (see Note)
- 2 garlic cloves, finely chopped
- 1 teaspoon chopped fresh ginger
- 1–2 dried red chilies, crumbled, or to taste
- 2 tablespoons fermented black beans, rinsed and drained

- 1 tablespoon soy sauce
- 2 teaspoons dry sherry or rice wine
- ¾ cup chicken broth
- 1 tablespoon vegetable or peanut oil
- 1 green onion, thinly sliced (optional)
- 1 tablespoon cornstarch mixed with ¼ cup cold water or chicken broth

Scrub the clams and mussels with a stiff brush and rinse under cold running water. Gently pull the beards off the mussels. Place the clams and mussels in separate large bowls and cover with cold water. You may do this step early in the day and refrigerate. Take the shellfish out of the refrigerator an hour before cooking.

In a bowl, mix the garlic, ginger, chilies, and fermented black beans.

Combine the soy sauce, dry sherry, and chicken broth in a bowl and set aside.

Drain the clams or mussels in a colander. Discard any that are not tightly closed or do not close tightly when rapped sharply on the countertop.

Place a wok over medium-high heat and heat the oil. Add the fermented black bean mixture and stir-fry for 30 seconds, then add the clams, mussels, and soy sauce mixture. Cover the wok and cook 5 minutes over high heat, or until all the shells pop open.

Sprinkle the green onion over the clams and mussels. Push the shells aside and stir the cornstarch mixture into the sauce. Continue cooking until the sauce has thickened. Discard any shells that have not opened, then toss to distribute the sauce and green onion well. Serve immediately.

NOTE: You can use all clams or all mussels if you prefer; use 2½ pounds of clams or 1¾ pounds mussels.

Squid Tossed with Soy Sauce and Oil

This very simple recipe is a wonderful showcase for the delicate, clean flavor of squid.

2 *pounds whole squid (about 1 pound cleaned)*

2 *teaspoons soy sauce*

2 *teaspoons vegetable or peanut oil*

Few drops of sesame oil (optional)

Place the squid, fin side down, on a cutting board. Cut the squid apart between the tentacles and eyes. Squeeze the base of the tentacles between your thumb and index finger to pop out and discard the round beak from the center. Rinse the tentacles.

Cut vertically through the top of the squid body and spread the body open. With the dull edge of your knife, scrape away and discard the innards, including the clear plasticlike cartilage. Rinse the squid bodies. You may remove the outer purple membrane, but it adds color and the squid is more flavorful if you leave it intact. The squid can be refrigerated for 6 or 8 hours at this point.

Open the body flat, with the inside face up. With a sharp knife, score lightly with 6 or 7 diagonal cuts in each direction to form a diamond pattern.

Fill a large saucepan two-thirds full with water and bring to a boil. Drop the squid into the water and cook about 1 minute over medium heat, stirring lightly with a wooden spoon or chopsticks. The squid bodies will curl up into cylinders with the diamond pattern facing out. You may check one for doneness by cutting through a squid body. It should be opaque all the way through. Do not overcook them or they will become tough. Drain the squid and shake out any excess water. Transfer to a serving bowl, and toss with the soy sauce, oil, and sesame oil, if using, and serve immediately.

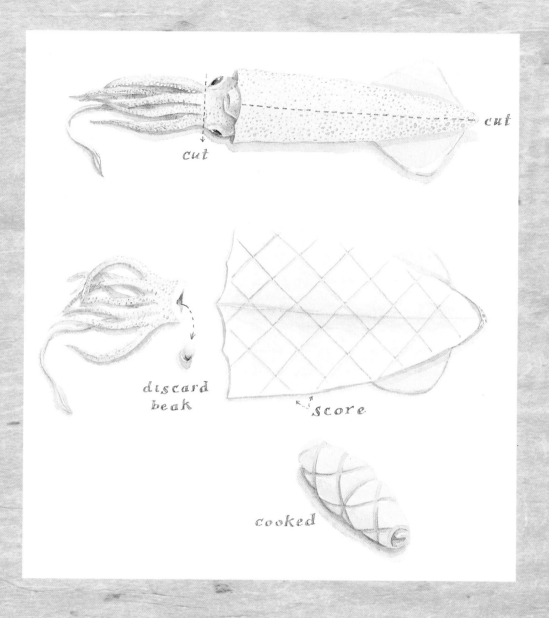

Simple Steamed Fish
with Variations

MAKES 4 TO 6 SERVINGS

Of all the fish recipes, this may be our favorite for bringing out the natural sweetness of fresh fish. The less you do, the more the fish's delicate flavor comes through. If the fish you choose is a stronger-flavored one, balance it with a pungent seasoning like garlic or ginger; see Variations.

1½–2   *pounds fish, preferably whole, such as red snapper, rock cod, large flounder, or black bass, or a thick chunk of striped or black bass*

1   *1½-inch piece ginger, peeled and cut in fine slivers*

1   *green onion, thinly sliced*

2   *cilantro sprigs, leaves only (optional)*

3   *tablespoons peanut oil*

4½   *teaspoons soy sauce*

Scale the fish if necessary and rinse it well. Pat dry, then place the fish in a heat-proof dish.

Set a rack in a pot and add water to a depth of 1½ to 2 inches. (If you are using a steamer, fill the lower tier half full with water.) Bring to a boil. Set the dish on the rack (or on the upper tier of the steamer) and steam over high heat for 15 to 20 minutes. (The cooking time will vary depending on the variety and thickness of the fish. Test for doneness by poking a chopstick or sharp knife through the thickest part of the fish. It should flake easily and look opaque all the way to the bone.)

When the fish is done, use a turkey baster or spoon to discard any liquid from the dish that has accumulated during steaming. Keep the fish warm.

Sprinkle the ginger, green onion, and cilantro, if using, over the fish. Heat the oil in a small skillet, then add the soy sauce and heat through a few seconds. Pour the hot oil mixture over the fish and serve immediately.

VARIATIONS

- **For a fish with a strong flavor**: Before steaming, top the fish with a ½-inch piece of ginger cut in thin rounds and green onion cut into 1-inch lengths; discard them after the fish is cooked. Double the quantities of ginger, green onion, and cilantro used in the main recipe and add 4½ teaspoons dry sherry or rice wine, 4½ teaspoons soy sauce, and ¼ teaspoon sugar to the hot oil.
- **Steamed Fish with Garlic**: Peel 1 to 2 garlic cloves and cut into slivers. Sprinkle the steamed fish with green onion and cilantro as above, but reserve the ginger. Heat 3 tablespoons peanut oil in a small skillet, then stir-fry the ginger and slivered garlic for 30 seconds. Add 4½ teaspoons dry sherry or rice wine, 4½ teaspoons soy sauce, and ¼ teaspoon sugar to the oil. Pour the hot oil mixture over the fish and serve.

Steamed Fish in Black Bean Sauce

This simple recipe blends the complex flavors of black beans and garlic perfectly. Use salmon, snapper, whole sand dabs, rock cod, or bass. Several variations follow.

1–1½	pounds fish	2	teaspoons dark soy sauce
	Salt	1	teaspoon light soy sauce
	Pepper	½	teaspoon sugar
1	garlic clove, finely chopped	1	1-inch piece ginger, peeled and cut in fine slivers
1	tablespoon fermented black beans, rinsed and drained	1	green onion, cut into ¼-inch pieces
1	teaspoon dry sherry or rice wine		

Wash the fish and pat dry. Lightly sprinkle the fish with salt and pepper. Arrange the fish in one layer in a heatproof dish; it should fit without crowding.

In a small bowl, combine the garlic, fermented black beans, dry sherry, soy sauces, and sugar and pour the mixture over the fish. Sprinkle the ginger and onion over the fish.

Set a rack in a pot and add water to a depth of 1½ to 2 inches. (If you are using a steamer, fill the lower tier half full with water.) Bring to a boil. Set the dish on the rack (or on the upper tier of the steamer) and steam for 15 to 25 minutes over high heat. (The cooking time will vary depending on the variety and thickness of

the fish. Test for doneness by poking a chopstick or sharp knife through the thickest part of the fish. It should flake easily and look opaque all the way to the bone.) Serve immediately.

VARIATIONS

+ **With Skate Wings**: Substitute skinned skate wings for the fish. Use poultry shears to cut the skate into 2 × 2-inch pieces. Proceed as above.
+ **With Prawns**: Substitute 1 pound medium prawns in the shell for the fish. With a sharp knife, cut each prawn through the shell just far enough to expose the sand vein down the back. Remove the sand vein. Rinse the prawns and shake off any excess moisture. (The prawns may be shelled but they will have less flavor.) Proceed as above.
+ **With Stir-Fried Ginger and Green Onion**: Do not add the ginger and green onion to the fish before cooking. Stir-fry the ginger and green onion in 5 teaspoons of vegetable or peanut oil for 30 seconds. Pour the mixture over the fish just before serving.
+ **With Garlic**: Omit the green onion and do not add the ginger to the fish before cooking. Mince 1 to 2 garlic cloves and stir-fry with the ginger in 5 teaspoons of vegetable or peanut oil for 30 seconds. Pour the mixture over the fish just before serving.

GARLIC   GINGER

GREEN ONION

Fish Every Night

ANNABEL

Father loved fish and seafood. We had it in some form as one of our courses every night. His day often began with a phone call to the fish market asking the proprietor, "What's fresh today?" A spirited discussion would follow. His standards were high; he described a fish that was less than fresh as "wearing glasses," meaning the eyes were already sunken from loss of moisture. If there wasn't anything fresh, we ate canned sardines. (In deference to him, the fish market continued to deliver fish to our house years after they stopped home delivery to other customers.)

Occasionally Father made his own salted fish and caviar. Whenever one of his fishermen friends shared a huge catch, Father dressed and salted the fish and roe, placing them in a contraption he devised out of clothes hangers and old curtains and hanging it on our backyard clothesline to cure. The bundle was visible to all the neighbors surrounding our tiny yard; they must have been curious about his method for drying curtains.

I especially loved Father's caviar and eagerly waited for it to be properly cured. As soon as Father said, "It's just right," I mixed the rich dark roe with my rice and savored every bite. It has been thirty years since I have tasted that delicacy, but the memory of it still lingers.

Hong Kong Cafe

ANNABEL

Father was co-owner and manager of Hong Kong Cafe, a Chinese restaurant in old downtown Sacramento that served both homestyle and banquet food, ranging from modest dishes like steamed minced pork to elegant dishes like abalone soup or sweet-and-sour fish.

Going to the restaurant was an adventure because the neighborhood was so different from the tree-lined street where I lived. In a window across the street lightbulbs spelled out the mysterious words BAIL BONDS. Our parents hurried us past a burlesque theater, but we still cast surreptitious glances at the photographs of buxom women dressed only in tassels. A neon-framed sign depicting happy diners marked the restaurant.

If we went in the kitchen entrance we were greeted by a confusion of hissing woks, clouds of steam, tantalizing aromas, shouted orders, and the rhythmic *chop-chop* of cleavers.

Outside the kitchen, purple jacquard curtains opened into a linoleum-floored dining room. Private curtained booths were available, each with a buzzer for summoning waiters. To prevent us from annoying the waiters, our parents told us the buzzer summoned the police. We used to dare each other to press it anyway to see if the police would really come, but not one of us was ever brave enough to try.

Starched cloths covered tables set with shot glasses filled with toothpicks, and cruets for soy sauce and condiments. Dusty landscapes in gilt frames covered the walls. A glossy dark wood wainscot was inset with contraptions where, for a few cents, diners could select the latest tunes to play on the jukebox while they ate the best chow mein in town.

In 1962, when Father was seventy-two years old, the restaurant closed. The restaurant refrigerator went into Esther's bedroom and the chairs were divided among our ever-growing family. Four of those chairs have traveled with me wherever I have moved; I like having a touch of Hong Kong Cafe in my home.

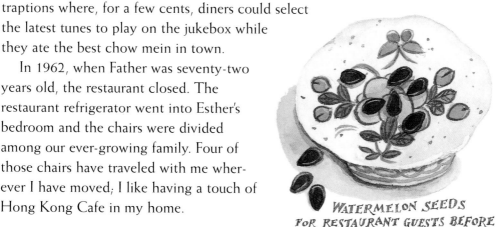

WATERMELON SEEDS
FOR RESTAURANT GUESTS BEFORE
THE FIRST COURSE

Sweet-and-Sour Whole Fish

Annabel's father occasionally prepared this fried whole fish topped with a colorful and tangy sauce for family parties. The fish made for a spectacular presentation. We were especially happy when he added mixed Chinese sweet pickles of carrots, ginger, cucumbers, and shallots. This dish can also be made with fish fillets.

1	1½- to 2-pound whole fish, such as rock cod or bass
¼	cup dry sherry or rice wine

SAUCE

1¼	cups water
¼	cup brown sugar
⅓	cup vinegar
1	tablespoon soy sauce, or to taste
1	teaspoon salt, or to taste
⅓	cup pineapple juice
2	tablespoons ketchup

1	egg
6–7	cups peanut oil for deep-frying
½	cup all-purpose flour

1	tablespoon vegetable or peanut oil for stir-frying
2	garlic cloves, minced
1	tablespoon minced fresh ginger
1	green onion, thinly sliced
1	carrot, cut in matchsticks
¼	green bell pepper, thinly sliced
¼	red pepper, thinly sliced
½	yellow onion, thinly sliced
7	ounces canned pineapple chunks in juice, juice reserved
½	cup mixed Chinese pickles (available in Asian grocery stores) cut in bite-sized pieces (optional)
2	tablespoons cornstarch mixed with ¼ cup water

Wash the fish and pat it dry. Cut the fish across the thickest parts in 2 or 3 places on each side, cutting almost to the bone. Marinate the fish in the dry sherry, turning it occasionally while you proceed.

In a medium bowl, combine the sauce ingredients. Break the egg into a large, deep dish and beat well. Set aside. Line a cookie sheet with several layers of paper towels and set aside.

Fill a wok or large Dutch oven with oil to within 2½ inches of the rim. (You may also want to line the floor with old newspapers.) Clip a candy thermometer to the side of the wok or Dutch oven, and heat the oil to 375°F. Dip the fish in the beaten egg to coat thoroughly. Put the flour in a large paper bag. Add the egg-dipped fish, hold the bag closed, and shake it gently until the fish is evenly coated. Shake off any excess flour. Carefully lower the fish into the oil and fry 7 to 8 minutes on each side, constantly ladling hot oil over the fish. The fish will immediately lower the temperature of the oil, so adjust the heat as necessary to maintain an oil temperature of 365°F. to 370°F. Remove the fish and drain on the prepared cookie sheet. Keep warm.

Place a skillet or another wok over medium-high heat and heat 1 tablespoon oil. Add the garlic, ginger, and green onion and cook for about 30 seconds. Add the carrot, bell peppers, and yellow onion and stir-fry for 5 minutes.

Add the sauce ingredients and bring to a boil. Stir in the pineapple chunks and Chinese pickles, then lower the heat and stir in the cornstarch mixture. Continue cooking until the sauce has thickened.

Transfer the fried fish to a large platter, spoon the sauce over the fish, and serve immediately.

VARIATION

Fried Fish Fillets: Substitute 2 pounds fish fillets, such as rock cod or bass, about 1 to 1½ inches thick, for the whole fish. Marinate and coat with egg and flour as above. Place a skillet or wok over high heat, then heat ¾ cup oil to about 370°F. Fry the fish about 5 to 7 minutes on each side. Remove the fish, drain on the prepared cookie sheet, and proceed.

Lobster Tails in Special Sauce

This makes a dramatic, beautiful banquet dish and it also stands on its own as an elegant main course with rice. You may substitute crab, shrimp, or scallops for the lobster.

2 garlic cloves, finely chopped	2 pounds lobster tails in the shell
4 ounces ground pork	1 tablespoon vegetable or peanut oil
1 tablespoon fermented black beans, rinsed and drained	1 green onion, cut into 1-inch pieces
1½ teaspoons soy sauce	¾ cup Simple Chicken Broth (page 19) or canned low-sodium chicken broth
1 teaspoon salt	2 teaspoons cornstarch mixed with ¼ cup cold water or chicken broth
⅛ teaspoon sugar	2 eggs, lightly beaten
1 tablespoon dry sherry or rice wine	

In a mixing bowl, combine the garlic, ground pork, fermented black beans, soy sauce, salt, sugar, and dry sherry. Chop the lobster tails into 1-inch pieces.

Place a wok over medium-high heat. Heat the oil, then add the pork mixture and cook it 2 to 3 minutes, breaking it up into small pieces with a spatula, until it is no longer pink.

Stir in the lobster pieces and cook until they turn bright orange and the lobster meat is opaque white, about 7 minutes. Add the green onion and chicken broth and bring to a boil. Stir in the cornstarch mixture and cook until the sauce has thickened.

With a spatula, clear a space on one side of the wok and pour in the eggs. Allow them to set about 1 minute, then gently mix into the lobster. Serve immediately.

✦ **With Prawns or Scallops or a Combination**: Substitute 1½ pounds peeled, deveined prawns or scallops or a mixture of the two for the lobster. Cook 3 minutes, or until the prawns are pink and opaque and the scallops are opaque.

✦ **With Crab**: Substitute a 2-pound cooked crab for the lobster. Remove the crabmeat from the shell, keeping the meat as intact as possible. For a more dramatic, colorful version, remove the crabmeat from the body and smaller leg sections only, reserving the largest leg and claw sections. With poultry shears, cut through the shell lengthwise along the edge of the leg sections and pry the shell partially open. Crack the claws with a nutcracker and remove any small, sharp bits of shell. Make the sauce as above, adding the crab during the last minute of cooking to heat through.

CRAB in SPECIAL SAUCE variation

Steamed Eggs with Clams

This is a savory custard. Boiling the water for this recipe is an essential step because it rids the water of tiny air bubbles that will ruin the silky texture of the custard.

4 eggs	1/4 teaspoon salt
1 6½-ounce can minced clams	1½ teaspoons oyster sauce
1½ cups water, boiled and cooled to lukewarm	1 green onion, very thinly sliced (optional)

In a mixing bowl, beat the eggs well with a fork. Drain the clams, reserving the clam liquid in a measuring cup. Add enough of the cooled water to the clam liquid to make 1¾ cups. Add to the eggs with the clams and the salt and stir until blended. Pour into a heatproof dish.

Set a rack in a pot and add water to a depth of 1½ to 2 inches. (If you are using a steamer, fill the lower tier half full with water.) Bring to a boil. Set the dish on the rack (or on the upper tier of the steamer). Lower the heat to a simmer and steam for 25 minutes. The eggs are done when they don't jiggle in the middle when the dish is tapped or an inserted toothpick comes out clean.

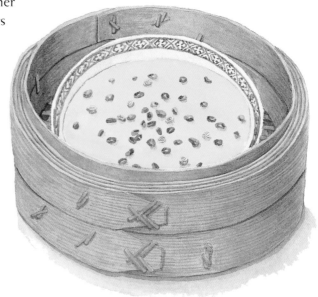

Pour the oyster sauce over the eggs and spread evenly over the surface with the bottom of a spoon. (A Chinese soup spoon works perfectly for this.) If desired, sprinkle with chopped green onion. Serve hot, with a serving spoon to spoon the eggs over rice.

CHOP CHOP: POULTRY

For a Chinese meal, poultry is never carved at the table; it is chopped in the kitchen into pieces the diners can manage with chopsticks. It is not considered impolite to chew the meat off the bone while holding a piece of chicken up to your mouth or even in your mouth with the chopsticks. There's even a term for this, *looe*. Using fingers, however, is bad form, so it's important to cut meat or poultry into fairly small pieces. Usually the cut-up poultry is reassembled on a platter to approximate its original shape.

The traditional tool of choice for cutting up poultry is a Chinese cleaver, which is excellent for hacking through bone. However, this makes for messy work and bones are prone to splintering. If you prefer, you may cheat by using poultry shears to cut through the bones once you have neatly sliced through the meat with a knife.

To prepare a chicken or other poultry for the table, follow these steps:

- ✦ Have an extra pan and a warm oval platter handy.
- ✦ Cut through the joint, wiggling the bones as you cut, to locate the connections: Cut off the drumsticks, then the wing tips, the second joints of the wings, the drumettes, and the thighs. Place these pieces in the extra pan.
- ✦ With a knife or poultry shears and the chicken breast side up, cut horizontally all the way up each side from the cavity to the clavicle bone. The breast is now separated from the back.

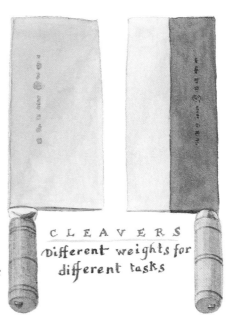

CLEAVERS
Different weights for different tasks

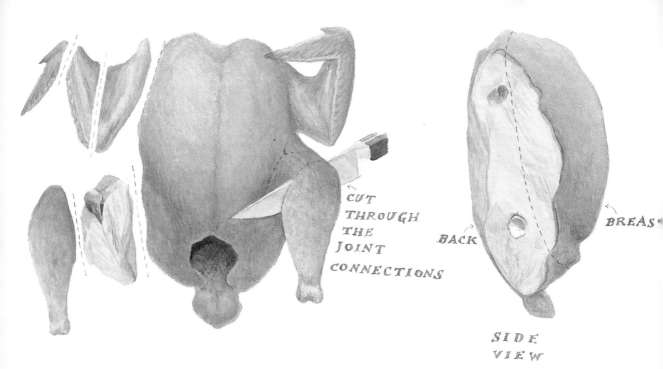

CUT THROUGH THE JOINT CONNECTIONS

SIDE VIEW

BACK

BREAST

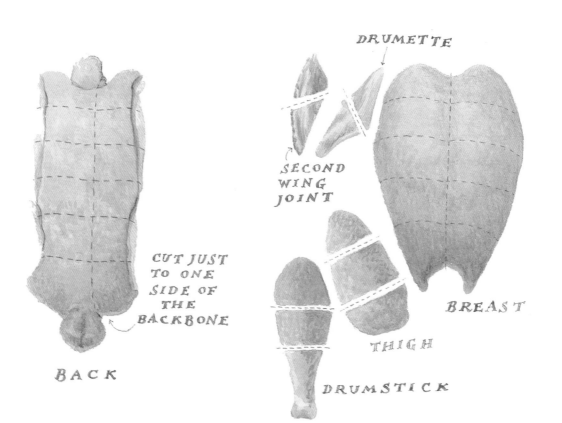

DRUMETTE

SECOND WING JOINT

CUT JUST TO ONE SIDE OF THE BACKBONE

BACK

BREAST

THIGH

DRUMSTICK

Start assembling pieces on the platter:

+ With a knife or poultry shears, cut lengthwise through the back, just to one side of the backbone. Turn the pieces bone side down and chop each piece crosswise into 5 or 6 pieces. Roughly reassemble the pieces, bone side down, in the center of the platter.
+ With the breast skin side up, cut lengthwise through the center of the breast. Poultry shears help cut through the bone.
+ Chop each halved breast crosswise into 5 or 6 pieces. Reassemble and arrange on top of the back pieces.
+ Chop the drumettes and second wing joints in half crosswise and lay alongside the breast pieces.
+ Chop the thigh pieces crosswise into 3 or 4 pieces. Reassemble and put at lower end of the breast pieces.
+ Chop the drumsticks crosswise into 2 or 3 pieces. Reassemble and put alongside the thigh pieces.

How Done Is Done?

To the Chinese palate, slightly undercooked chicken is considered *gobt,* or pleasantly smooth. However, in the recipes that follow we have modified the traditional cooking times both to appeal to non-Chinese tastes and because we are mindful of minimum safe cooking times and temperatures. You may prefer to cook poultry even longer. Use your judgment and cook according to your taste.

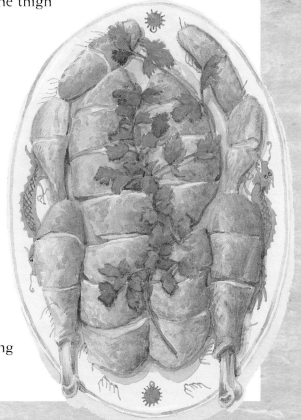

Roast chicken

Ellen's mother says she misses roast chicken now, which she always made for her children's trips home from college. We can't ever make it taste as good as hers, so the secret ingredient must have been the company.

1   4½- to 5½-pound chicken, preferably a roaster (see Note)

1½ teaspoons salt

1½ teaspoons chopped fresh ginger

3   tablespoons soy sauce

1   tablespoon dry sherry or rice wine

¼   teaspoon sugar

Pinch of Chinese five-spice powder

1   celery stalk, cut into 3 or 4 pieces

1   small yellow onion, peeled and quartered

2½ teaspoons cornstarch mixed with ¼ cup cold water or chicken broth

Cilantro, for garnish (optional)

Preheat the oven to 375°F. Set a rack in a shallow roasting pan. Pour about 3 cups water into the pan, to just below the level of the rack.

Rinse the chicken and pat it dry. Rub it with the salt inside and out. Place the chicken on the rack, breast side up.

In a bowl, combine the ginger, soy sauce, dry sherry, sugar, and five-spice powder. Rub the mixture all over the inside and outside of the chicken, letting the excess drip into the pan. Stuff the celery and onion loosely into the cavity.

Roast the chicken about 2 to 2½ hours, basting 2 or 3 times with the pan juices. Test for doneness by piercing the thigh with a knife; the juices should run clear. Transfer the chicken to a cutting board and let it rest for 10 minutes.

Chop the chicken into serving pieces (pages 109–111) and reassemble on a serving platter. Cover the chicken loosely with foil and keep warm in a 200°F. oven.

Strain the pan juices through a sieve into a small saucepan. Skim off and discard as much fat as possible. Bring the sauce to a boil. Lower the heat and stir in the cornstarch mixture. Continue cooking until the sauce has thickened.

Pour a thin layer of sauce over the chicken and garnish with the cilantro. Serve the remaining sauce on the side.

NOTE: A 3½- to 4½-pound fryer will take about 1¾ to 2 hours to cook.

Birthday Parties

As our family grew, so did the number of birthday parties we held. Aside from these family gatherings, almost all of the men worked seven days a week. Taking time off was not usually an option. Parties, however, provided an excuse for a day to relax together, and they were perpetuated by the need to reciprocate.

Milestone adult birthdays were observed with a special restaurant banquet; all other birthdays, whether for adults or children, were occasions to invite relatives to the house for lunch and dinner and for a long day of mah-jongg. Children were left to amuse themselves, do homework, or baby-sit the toddlers in hopes of a small tip from a lucky mah-jongg-playing parent.

For these occasions menus were written down, then revised. Days were spent in preparation. We children were assigned tasks suited to our small hands, including scouring teapots, picking feathers out of dried birds' nests, cleaning odd bits out of dried shrimp, and shelling and skinning walnuts. The house was cleaned, card tables were set out, and folding chairs were dragged out from storage under our beds.

We were often awakened by the smell of *lek doi,* Chinese doughnuts, sizzling in hot peanut oil. Breakfast was eaten amid tubs of marinating garlicky chicken and drying squabs, their heads lolling over the rim of a colander.

Lunch might include piles of fried chicken, barbecued spareribs, pork buns, platters heaped with chow mein, and plates of steaming dim sum. Later, influenced by American cooking, potato salad, barbecued hot dogs and hamburgers, Jell-O, and brown-and-serve rolls were added to the menu. Birthday cake and ice cream followed, with second helpings doled out midafternoon to the mah-jongg players, who by then were in need of a break.

Dinners were more elaborate. All afternoon, various meats, fish, and poultry were sliced and marinated. Vegetables were washed and chopped. Soups were set to simmer. Chickens were roasted. Children were responsible for setting tables, cleaning dishes, making tea, pulling strings off pea pods, and pinching the threadlike tails off bean sprouts.

Just before dinner, the kitchen would erupt with activity. Children delivering individual bowls of soup to each place setting wove through parents busy at chopping blocks, woks, ovens, steamers, and pots. Dish after dish was rushed to the tables so that everything would still be hot when we sat down.

Dinner might include shark's fin soup, stir-fried prawns and scallops with green loofah squash, pan-fried prawns in a sweet ketchup sauce, soy sauce squab, stuffed boned duck, lobster tails in special sauce, white-cooked chicken with dry-cured ham tucked under the skin, oyster beef with broccoli, and a whole fish, fried crisp and covered with a sweet-and-sour sauce.

Even after such a large lunch and midafternoon snacking, appetites were always primed for such feasts. Afterward, an especially exciting game of mah-jongg might continue late into the night, once or twice lasting until dawn. The last tile thrown, the children, fast asleep on all available beds, sofas, and chairs, were roused and taken home.

Batter-Fried Chicken

MAKES 3 POUNDS (ABOUT 10 TO 12 PIECES. ALLOW 2 OR 3 PIECES PER PERSON.)

This was *the* lunch staple at all our birthday parties. The garlicky marinade distinguishes this chicken from its American cousin.

1   3½-pound chicken, cut into serving pieces (see Note)

4   teaspoons chopped fresh ginger

3   garlic cloves, finely chopped

2   teaspoons salt

1½ teaspoons sugar

1   tablespoon soy sauce

1   teaspoon dry sherry or rice wine

1   cup all-purpose flour

½   cup cornstarch

½   teaspoon baking powder

1¼ cups water

6–7 cups peanut oil for deep-frying

Cut the chicken breasts in half, then cross-wise into 2 or 3 pieces. Separate the drumsticks from the thighs. Separate the drumettes from the other part of the wings. Reserve the other wing parts, backs, and necks for another use.

Combine the ginger, garlic, 1 1/2 teaspoons salt, sugar, soy sauce, and dry sherry in a baking pan. Toss the chicken pieces with the mixture to coat them well and marinate 2 to 3 hours in the refrigerator.

In a large mixing bowl, beat the flour, cornstarch, baking powder, 1/2 teaspoon salt, and water until smooth. Line a cookie sheet with several layers of paper towels.

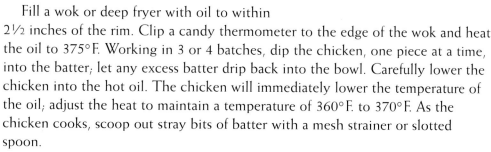

Fill a wok or deep fryer with oil to within 2 1/2 inches of the rim. Clip a candy thermometer to the edge of the wok and heat the oil to 375°F. Working in 3 or 4 batches, dip the chicken, one piece at a time, into the batter; let any excess batter drip back into the bowl. Carefully lower the chicken into the hot oil. The chicken will immediately lower the temperature of the oil; adjust the heat to maintain a temperature of 360°F. to 370°F. As the chicken cooks, scoop out stray bits of batter with a mesh strainer or slotted spoon.

Turn the chicken to brown evenly, cooking about 20 to 25 minutes (dark meat will take slightly longer than light meat). Remove the chicken pieces with a mesh strainer or slotted spoon and drain them on the prepared cookie sheet.

Serve hot.

NOTE: You can use any combination of drumsticks, thighs, breasts, and wings.

chinese chicken salad

Originally, the shredded chicken for this salad was deep-fried until it was slightly crispy. In this less rich version, boneless chicken breasts are baked and shredded. The salad was always made with iceberg lettuce, although romaine may be used instead. The pungent flavors of cilantro and oyster sauce predominate in this salad. Fried wonton wrappers provide contrast to the other textures. A cup of roasted salted cashews may be used instead of wonton wrappers if you prefer to avoid frying altogether.

1½ pounds skinless, boneless chicken breast	**FOR THE DRESSING**
½ teaspoon salt	4 teaspoons hoisin sauce
⅛ teaspoon Chinese five-spice powder	2 tablespoons oyster sauce
1 tablespoon sesame seeds	½ teaspoon soy sauce
1 green onion, finely chopped	3 tablespoons sesame oil
½ head iceberg or romaine lettuce, shredded	1 tablespoon peanut oil
1½ cups loosely packed cilantro leaves, roughly chopped	⅛ teaspoon white pepper
	2 cups peanut oil for deep-frying
	¼ pound wonton wrappers

Preheat the oven to 350°F. Rub the chicken with the salt and Chinese five-spice powder. Place the chicken on a rack in a baking pan and bake for 50 minutes to 1 hour, until cooked through. Let cool 10 minutes. Using 2 forks, shred the meat. Set aside.

Place a nonstick skillet over medium heat. Add the sesame seeds to the dry skillet and toast them until they are lightly browned, shaking the pan gently, about 2 minutes. Remove the sesame seeds immediately to cool. (Leaving them in the hot skillet may cause them to burn.)

Combine the green onion, lettuce, and cilantro in a large serving bowl, cover, and refrigerate.

In a small bowl, combine the hoisin sauce, oyster sauce, soy sauce, sesame oil, peanut oil, and white pepper and mix well. Line a cookie sheet with several layers of paper towels and set aside.

Pour the oil for deep-frying into a wide, deep skillet. Clip on a candy thermometer and heat the oil to 365°F.

While the oil is heating, place the stack of wonton wrappers on a cutting board. With a sharp knife or cleaver, cut through all the layers into ¼-inch strips. Separate the layers with your fingers, making sure that the strips are not sticking together.

Divide the strips into 4 batches. Carefully put the first batch into the oil and separate the strips with a long-handled wooden spoon or long chopsticks. The strips should sizzle and twist immediately; they will be done in about 20 to 30 seconds. Remove them with a slotted spoon or wire mesh strainer and drain on the prepared cookie sheet. Repeat with the remaining batches.

Add the shredded chicken to the lettuce mixture, then add the dressing and toss. Taste and add more oyster sauce, hoisin sauce, or sesame oil, if necessary. Toss in the wonton strips and toasted sesame seeds. Serve immediately. (The wonton strips will not remain crisp for long in the dressing. You may prepare the ingredients separately up to 1 hour ahead of time, but do not assemble them until the last minute.)

CHINESE CHICKEN SALAD with CASHEWS

chicken in Foil or Parchment

Children love opening these festive surprise packets. This is a great dish to make for a dinner party because it can be assembled ahead of time and popped into the oven about half an hour before dinner. Be sure to open the packets over a bowl of rice to soak up the sauce. In the variation, ginger is omitted, and hoisin sauce and longer baking give the chicken a slightly caramelized glaze.

MARINADE

- 1 tablespoon peeled and chopped fresh ginger
- ½ teaspoon salt
- 2 tablespoons soy sauce
- 1 teaspoon dry sherry or rice wine
- 2 tablespoons oyster sauce
- ½ teaspoon sugar

- ⅛ teaspoon sesame oil
- 1 teaspoon red bean curd
- ⅛ teaspoon Chinese five-spice powder
- 1 tablespoon vegetable or peanut oil

- 1½ pounds skinless, boneless chicken thighs, cut into 1½-inch chunks (see Note)

Fold each square in half

Cut sixteen 6-inch squares from aluminum foil or parchment. If you are using foil, fold each square in half into a rectangle. Make two ¼-inch folds on each short side, leaving the long side open. Do not prefold the parchment.

Combine the marinade ingredients in a medium bowl and mix well.

Leave open

¼"

Double-fold the short sides

Add the chicken, toss together, and marinate in the refrigerator for 1 to 2 hours.

Preheat the oven to 350° F.

Put 2 pieces of chicken into each foil packet and double fold the open edge tightly to seal in the juices. If you are using parchment, place the

Put 2 pieces chicken into each foil packet. Double-fold the open edge.

chicken chunks in the center of each square. Fold the parchment in half over the chicken and double fold all three open edges tightly, pinching and crimping to seal securely.

Lay the packets in a single layer on jelly roll pans or cookie sheets. Bake for 25 to 30 minutes for thigh meat, 20 to 25 minutes for breast meat. Open a packet and cut through a piece of chicken to test for doneness; it should be opaque and no longer pink. Bake a few minutes longer if necessary. Serve hot.

NOTE: Skinless, boneless thigh meat is available at most supermarkets. You can substitute breast meat, but it will be drier.

VARIATION

With Hoisin Sauce: Follow the procedures as above, but use the following ingredients in the marinade and increase the baking time to 35 to 40 minutes for thigh meat, 20 to 25 minutes for breast meat.

1½	teaspoons hoisin sauce	¾	teaspoon salt
⅛	teaspoon Chinese five-spice powder	⅛	teaspoon black or white pepper
4	teaspoons oyster sauce	¼	teaspoon sesame oil
1	tablespoon soy sauce	1½	teaspoons cornstarch
1½	teaspoons sugar	4	teaspoons vegetable or peanut oil

Steamed Chicken with Cloud Ears and Black Mushrooms

MAKES 4 TO 6 SERVINGS AS PART OF A CHINESE MEAL

For such a simply prepared dish, this is remarkably flavorful. Skinless, boneless chicken is not traditional but is lighter.

2 tablespoons dried cloud ears

20 tiger lily buds

4–5 black mushrooms

1 pound chicken breasts, thighs, or drumsticks, or ¾ pound skinless, boneless breast or thigh meat

1 teaspoon dry sherry or rice wine

1 teaspoon oyster sauce

1 teaspoon light soy sauce

1 teaspoon dark soy sauce

½ teaspoon sugar

1 teaspoon cornstarch

¼ teaspoon salt

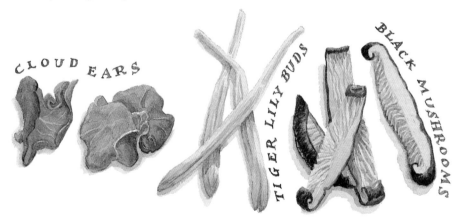

CLOUD EARS

TIGER LILY BUDS

BLACK MUSHROOMS

In separate bowls, rinse, then soak the cloud ears, tiger lily buds, and mushrooms in hot water to cover for 30 to 45 minutes.

Meanwhile, cut the chicken into pieces small enough to be eaten with chopsticks: cut the thighs and drumsticks in half, halve the breasts, and cut each half crosswise into 3 or 4 pieces. Discard any sharp bone fragments. Arrange the chicken in a single layer in a heatproof dish. Combine the remaining ingredients, pour over the chicken, and mix well.

Rinse and drain the cloud ears, tiger lily buds, and mushrooms. Cut off any hard parts from the cloud ears. Cut off the hard ends of the tiger lily buds. Squeeze the mushrooms dry and cut off and discard the stems. Cut the caps into ¼-inch slices. Scatter the cloud ears, tiger lily buds, and mushrooms over the chicken.

Set a rack in a pot and add water to a depth of 1½ to 2 inches. (If you are using a steamer, fill the lower tier half full with water.) Bring to a boil. Set the dish on the rack (or on the upper tier of a steamer) and steam for 20 minutes over high heat, or until the chicken is cooked through. Serve hot.

VARIATION

Salted Steamed Chicken: This even easier dish has a different flavor and is not strictly a variation, but the cutting and steaming procedures are the same. Use:

- 1¼ pounds chicken, as above
- 1 teaspoon salt
- 1 1-inch piece ginger, peeled and cut in thin strips
- 1½ teaspoons vegetable or peanut oil
- 1 green onion, cut in thin slivers (optional)
- 1 tablespoon coarsely chopped cilantro leaves (optional)

Cut the chicken as above. The night before or early the same day, salt the chicken, place it in a shallow dish, cover, and refrigerate.

When ready to cook the chicken, rinse off the salt well and shake off any excess water. Place the chicken in a heatproof dish and toss with the ginger and oil.

Steam as above. Discard some of the liquid that has accumulated around the chicken during steaming. Sprinkle with the green onion and cilantro, if desired, and serve hot.

SALTED STEAMED CHICKEN without skin

Tales of Two Chopsticks

ELLEN

Because of our lack of English skills, Annabel and I were quiet in kindergarten. One day, though, the teacher brought out a pair of chopsticks to show different ways people eat. Annabel and I felt all eyes turn to us. Chopsticks were familiar; we had learned to use them before we were ever given forks. The teacher handed the chopsticks to me to demonstrate and I was eager to show off my ability. Unfortunately, her choice of "food" was a large polished wooden bead, which, of course, slipped repeatedly. I felt mortified and fraudulent. Annabel had no better luck. Without language to explain the problem, we must have left the other children wondering if we secretly ate with our hands at home.

Far from that, we were succumbing to a new influence in the family. An uncle had just married a beautiful woman with sophisticated Hong Kong ways. She was the first woman in the family I ever saw sleep late.

One etiquette tip she shared with us was that it was considered more refined to hold one's chopsticks near the top and we had to agree it looked more graceful. We were still struggling to keep our fingers out of gravy at this point, grasping our chopsticks so close to the bottom tips. Valiantly we worked to copy her technique until our chopsticks were long bird legs wandering about our food.

Unfortunately, we could only snatch small morsels this way and

A CHOPSTICK HOLDER TACKED ON A CUPBOARD DOOR

our hands soon crept back down toward the less affected middle. Appetite won over elegance.

Still, however I manipulated chopsticks, they felt more natural than a fork, which balanced awkwardly in my hand. Its sharp points clicked coldly against my teeth. It wasn't until I checked out an etiquette book at the library in fourth or fifth grade that I learned about how to use a knife and fork properly—to keep switching hands when using a knife and fork, or keep the knife in the right hand and eat from a fork with the left hand, but only if it is held tines down—something called European style. Utensils had to be set a certain way, used in proper order, and left just so on the right plates. So many distracting techniques to remember!

I insist that food tastes better with chopsticks. And although I've seen relatives use chopsticks to rapidly shovel rice from bowls held up to their lips like trucks backed up to loading docks, chopsticks generally force us to eat at a slower pace. Listen in a restaurant sometime. Chopsticks don't clatter.

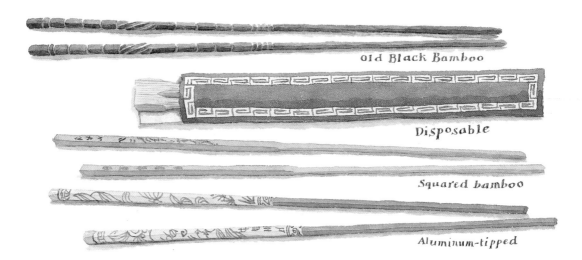

Old Black Bamboo

Disposable

Squared bamboo

Aluminum-tipped

walnut or cashew chicken

In November, a bombardment of black walnuts on the roof all night announced that it was time to pick the windfalls for Christmas money. Black walnuts require a deft touch with a hammer to crack the extremely thick, hard shells to get to the oily, strongly flavored nutmeat. It wasn't worth it. We were happy to fill twenty large burlap sacks full and sell them for a dollar a sack.

Our rarer English walnuts could bring five dollars a sack, but since English walnuts have thinner shells and large, mild nutmeats, we kept them for sweets or walnut chicken—not an everyday dish because of the effort required to shell and skin the walnuts, but a popular dish at birthday dinners. Instead of walnuts, you can substitute roasted salted cashews or blanched toasted almonds, which don't require advance preparation, or you can omit the step of frying the walnuts if you prefer.

1½ cups walnuts

1 pound skinless, boneless chicken, either breast or thigh meat

MARINADE

¼ teaspoon salt

1 tablespoon soy sauce

½ teaspoon dry sherry or rice wine

¼ teaspoon sugar

2 cups peanut oil for deep-frying (optional)

3–4 ounces snow peas, strings removed and cut in half on the diagonal

1 carrot, peeled and thinly sliced on the diagonal

1 tablespoon vegetable or peanut oil

⅓ cup Simple Chicken Broth (page 19) or canned low-sodium chicken broth

1 tablespoon oyster sauce, or to taste

2 teaspoons cornstarch mixed with ¼ cup chicken broth

Preheat the oven to 300°F. Spread the walnuts out in a single layer on a cookie sheet and toast them about 15 minutes. Remove the skins, using a toothpick or nut pick to help. You do not have to remove all of the skin, but it will impart a slightly bitter flavor to the dish. When cooled, store the walnuts in an airtight container. (You can do this up to 1 week ahead.)

Cut the chicken into $1/2 \times 1/2 \times 1 1/2$-inch strips. Mix the marinade ingredients in a bowl. Add the chicken, mix well, and marinate for 30 minutes.

Heat the oil in a deep skillet to 360°F. Deep-fry the skinned walnuts until browned, about 30 seconds. Remove the walnuts with a slotted spoon and drain them on several layers of paper towels. (This step is optional.)

Put 3 cups water in a small saucepan and bring it to a boil. Add the snow peas and carrot and blanch for 1 minute. Drain them in a colander and rinse them under cold water to stop the cooking.

Place a wok over medium-high heat and heat 1 tablespoon oil. Stir-fry the chicken pieces until brown, about 3 minutes. Add the chicken broth and the oyster sauce and lower the heat to medium. Cook the chicken through, about 3 to 4 minutes. Add the cornstarch mixture and cook until the sauce has thickened. Add the snow peas and carrots and heat through. Stir in the walnuts. Serve immediately.

ENGLISH WALNUT LEAF

Stand Back Chicken (Braised Chicken)

Whenever Annabel's mother cooked this dish, the kitchen would be full of sizzling sounds and wonderful fragrances. Annabel's sister Esther took detailed notes when observing her mother cook this dish, and the name of this recipe comes from Esther's note to "stand back" after putting the chicken into the wok. Some versions of the recipe call for a cup of oil in the wok, but that requires standing back *and* covering the floor with newspapers. We find this version rich enough as is.

1	3½- to 4½-pound chicken (see Note)		1	teaspoon sugar
1	teaspoon salt		2	teaspoons vegetable or peanut oil
1½	teaspoons whiskey		1½	teaspoons chopped fresh ginger
2½	teaspoons soy sauce		1	green onion, thinly sliced
⅛	teaspoon pepper		¾	cups water

Rinse the chicken and pat it dry. Rub the chicken inside and out with the salt and set aside.

In a small bowl, mix the whiskey, soy sauce, pepper, and sugar. Set aside. Place a heavy Dutch oven or wok over medium-high heat and heat the oil. Put the chicken on its side into the Dutch oven or wok and stand back. (The oil may spatter.) Cook, uncovered, 3 to 4 minutes.

Turn the chicken onto its other side to brown, 3 to 4 minutes. Turn the chicken onto its back and brown, 3 to 4 minutes. Turn the chicken breast side down and brown, 3 to 4 minutes. If necessary, cook the chicken a few minutes longer wherever it is not evenly browned. Turn the chicken on its back.

Add the ginger and green onion to the pan. Pour the whiskey mixture over the chicken and cook, covered, for 15 seconds. Add the water, cover the pan, lower the heat to medium-low, and cook for 5 or 6 minutes.

Turn the chicken on one side and lower the heat to a simmer. Cook, covered, 8 to 10 minutes. Turn the chicken over on the other side and cook, covered, 8 to

10 minutes. Test for doneness by piercing the inner thigh with a sharp knife; the juices should run clear. If not, cook a few minutes longer.

Remove the chicken to a cutting board, letting the juices drain back into the pan. Cut the chicken into serving pieces and arrange on a serving platter. Pour the pan juices into a bowl, skim off the fat, and pour over the chicken.

NOTE: For a leaner version, you may skin the chicken first. Increase the oil for the wok to 1 tablespoon.

Father was larger than life to me. I loved to listen to the restaurant stories he told. At the Los Angeles restaurant he owned before I was born, movie stars such as Lucille Ball, Johnny Weissmuller, and Joan Crawford were customers. "Joan was always going on a diet. She was so worried about her weight," he loved to tell us. Or "Johnny Weissmuller loved my sweet-and-sour." Not that Father was any less colorful than his patrons. Once he shot a customer in the leg when he refused to pay. Rather than winding up in jail, Father went to court and got the case dismissed. He began by addressing the judge as "My young man," since the judge appeared young, then proceeded to talk about the indignity of having someone try to get away without paying and adding insult to injury by calling him a Chinaman. It was a miracle he didn't go to jail. He was fearless that way. I believe we get our pride from Father.

Father had such style with food. I remember watching him make radish roses, stuffing a whole boneless fish, or doing elegant things even with simple food. When he set fried oysters on a plate, they were nestled in a bed of shredded lettuce. The walnuts in his Walnut Chicken dish were pure gold because he meticulously removed the thin skin from each walnut before deep-frying them. Even when he packed sandwiches for our lunches, he was creative; he would give us each half of a chicken sandwich and half of a *char siu* sandwich for variety.

Such standards he set! Even as a child, I knew what he did with food was special and that no one was his equal in the kitchen.

I REMEMBER BEING VERY YOUNG AND WATCHING HIM MAKE RADISH ROSES...

Low Hop Joe's Soy Sauce chicken with variations

Annabel's father was famous for his soy sauce chicken. His recipe tasted different from any other. People would rhapsodize about the beautiful color and the subtle flavors. For Annabel, the Christmas holiday brings to mind the smell of soy sauce chicken cooking, as her father made numerous soy sauce chickens for their friends. Annabel finds herself doing the same thing now, giving them as gifts when she visits friends. The sauce can be made up to 1 month ahead. Once you have the sauce on hand, this is a very fast and easy recipe. The sauce can be reused to cook up to 4 whole chickens (see Note).

4   whole cardamom pods

2   cinnamon sticks or cassia bark pieces

1   tablespoon dried licorice root slices

5   star anise
     A few anise seeds

2   tablespoons whole cloves

1   9-inch-square piece of clean white
     muslin or cheesecloth

     White cotton string

4   pounds rock sugar

1   gallon soy sauce (thin or Kikkoman)
     (see Note)

1   3½- to 4½-pound chicken

Crack the cardamom pods and cinnamon sticks or cassia bark with a nutcracker or hammer. Combine the cardamom, cinnamon or cassia bark, licorice, star anise, anise seeds, and cloves and put them in the center of the muslin. Gather up the edges of the muslin and tie tightly with string.

Break the rock sugar into small pieces. Combine the rock sugar and soy sauce

LICORICE
ROOT

STAR ANISE

SZECHUAN
PEPPERCORNS

CLOVES

CASSIA
BARK

CARDAMOM
PODS

in a pot and heat over medium heat until the sugar dissolves. Add the spice bag, cover the pot, and bring to a boil. Add the chicken, using all of the sauce.

Cook the chicken over medium heat, uncovered, skimming off any foam as it accumulates. Turn the chicken every 10 minutes or so to cook it evenly. Cook the chicken for about 40 minutes to 1½ hours, depending on the size of the chicken.

Transfer the chicken to a serving platter and let cool 30 minutes. Cut the chicken into serving pieces and arrange on the platter (see pages 109–111). The chicken is usually served at room temperature, but it can be served hot or cold.

NOTE: The sauce may be used again for 2 or 3 more chickens; it will darken with each use. Once it has been used, store the sauce in clean quart jars, refrigerated, up to a week. Before reusing, discard any fat that has risen to the top and hardened. Unused sauce may be stored in the refrigerator for 2 weeks or frozen.

VARIATIONS

+ **Boneless Chicken Breasts**: Bring 1 quart sauce to a boil and add up to 6 boneless chicken breasts. As a main course, allow 1 per person. (You may remove the skin before cooking. The result will be less fatty and slightly saltier.) Lower the heat and simmer to the desired doneness, about 20 minutes.
+ **Game Hens**: Bring 1½ to 2 quarts sauce to a boil in a large pot and add up to 4 game hens. Lower the heat and simmer to the desired doneness, about 30 to 45 minutes. As part of a Chinese meal, allow ½ game hen per person.
+ **Chicken Wings or Drumettes**: Bring 1 quart sauce to a boil and add 1½ to 3 pounds chicken wings or drumettes. Lower the heat and simmer until cooked through, about 10 to 15 minutes. As part of a Chinese meal, allow 3 to 4 chicken wings or drumettes per person.
+ **Garlic and Orange-Flavored Soy Sauce Game Hens**: Combine 2 garlic cloves, 2 whole star anise, and 2 pieces of ginger, each 1 inch long, and put them in the center of a 6-inch square of muslin. Gather up the edges of the muslin and tie tightly with string. Break up 1 pound rock sugar into small pieces. Combine the spice bag, peel of ½ orange, 7 cups soy sauce, 5 cups water, and 1 pound rock sugar in a large enamel pot. Bring the mixture to a boil and simmer for 30 minutes. Add 2 whole game hens, lower the heat, and simmer, uncovered, to the desired doneness, about 30 to 45 minutes. This sauce can also be used for any of the variations listed above.

Boned Stuffed Duck (Pa Wong Op)

Annabel's father was renowned for this succulent, tender boned stuffed duck. Although it is a banquet dish, it is rarely found on restaurant menus because of the care and time involved. The first time Annabel thought of making *Pa Wong Op*, she felt over-whelmed just looking at the notes for this dish, which requires five to six hours of preparation. When she finally took a breath and started working, however, she said it was as if her father was suddenly in the kitchen guiding her. Don't be afraid to try this; while it takes time, it is not actually as complicated as it seems at first.

- 1   4- to 5-pound duck
- 1   tablespoon plus 1 teaspoon soy sauce
- 2   teaspoons dry sherry or rice wine
- 5   dried black mushrooms
- 1   1 × ¾-inch piece dried tangerine peel (see Glossary) (optional)
- 6–7   cups peanut oil for deep frying
- ½   cup bamboo shoots, cut in matchsticks
- 1   green onion, cut into 3 pieces
- 1   ¼-inch piece ginger, peeled and halved
- 1   celery stalk, cut into 3 pieces
- 2   whole star anise
- 1   teaspoon salt
- ¼   teaspoon sugar
- 4   salted preserved eggs (page 47)
- 4   ounces char siu (pages 136–137), cut in matchsticks
- 1   tablespoon cornstarch mixed with 1 tablespoon water

  Few cilantro sprigs, for garnish

Wash the duck well and pat it dry. Remove the fat from the cavity.

In a small bowl, combine 1 tablespoon soy sauce and 1 teaspoon of the dry sherry. Rub the duck inside and out with the mixture and marinate for 1 hour.

Meanwhile, put the black mushrooms in a small bowl with hot water to cover. Let stand 30 to 45 minutes to soften. Cut off and discard the hard stems. Rinse the caps, squeeze them dry, and cut into thin slices.

Put the tangerine peel in a small bowl and cover with hot water. Let stand 15 minutes. Drain.

Line a cookie sheet with several layers of paper towels and set aside.

Fill a wok or pan large and deep enough to fry the duck, with oil to within 2½ to 3 inches below the rim. (You may also want to line the floor with newspapers.) Clip a candy thermometer to the side of the wok or pan and heat the oil to 370° F. over medium heat. With a large strainer, carefully lower the duck into the oil, breast side up. The duck will immediately lower the temperature of the oil. Adjust the heat to maintain an oil temperature of 350° F. to 360° F. Deep-fry for 2 minutes, ladling hot oil over the duck the entire time. Using 2 strainers, turn the duck over very carefully. (Do not use a utensil that might pierce the skin.) Fry the second side for 2 minutes and repeat the procedure until the duck is golden brown all over, about 8 to 10 minutes.

Remove the duck and let it drain breast side down on the prepared cookie sheet. Let cool 15 to 20 minutes.

Meanwhile, in a large bowl, combine the bamboo shoots, green onion, ginger, celery, mushrooms, tangerine peel, star anise, salt, remaining 1 teaspoon dry sherry, and sugar.

Put the duck, breast side down, in a heatproof dish. With poultry shears or a sharp knife, split the duck along the backbone. Spoon the bamboo shoot mixture into the cavity.

Set a rack in a large pot (or flat-bottomed covered roasting pan large enough to hold the duck) and add water to just below the top of the rack. (If you are using a steamer, fill the lower tier three-fourths full with water.) Bring to a boil. Set the dish on the rack (or upper tier of a steamer) and steam 1½ to 2 hours over

Stuff after deep~frying

high heat, replenishing the pot with boiling water as necessary about every 20 to 30 minutes. Watch carefully to be sure the pan does not go dry. The duck is done if you can remove a rib bone at the back without much resistance.

Crack the salted preserved eggs one at a time into a small bowl. Pick out the yolks and rinse under cold water. The yolks should be firm and bright orange, and the eggs should have a briny odor. If a yolk is soft and mustard-colored, and the white is gray or black and has a strong odor, the egg has spoiled and should be discarded. Discard the whites. Cut the yolks in half.

Remove the duck from the steamer and let it rest until it is cool enough to handle, about 15 to 20 minutes. Remove the mixture from the inside. Reserve the bamboo shoots and mushrooms and discard the other ingredients. Drain the duck liquid, skim off the fat, and set the defatted liquid aside. If you are making this ahead, you may cover and refrigerate the liquid, then discard the hardened fat.

Leaving the duck in the dish breast side down, remove the bones. Start from the backbone area, moving toward the breast bones. Twist the joints apart at the wing and drumstick from the inside, being careful to leave the skin intact. Leave the leg and wing bones in. Remove some of the duck meat, leaving the outer layer of breast, drumstick, and wing meat intact. (Try to maintain the shape of the duck.) Shred the meat, mix it with the reserved bamboo shoots, mushrooms, and *char siu*, and spread the mixture evenly inside the cavity. Distribute the egg yolks evenly over the mixture, and press them gently into the stuffing. Pull the duck skin smoothly over the mixture; you will not be able to cover the mixture completely. (You can cover and refrigerate the duck at this point. Remove the duck from the refrigerator 1½ to 2 hours before serving.)

Bone

Set up the steaming pan or steamer as before. Steam the duck until the egg yolks are cooked through, about 45 minutes. (Test by cutting into a yolk with a knife.) Invert a large serving platter over the dish. Using oven mitts, hold the platter and dish together firmly and flip them over. Lift the dish off. Pour off any liquid that has collected into a saucepan.

Add the reserved defatted duck liquid to the saucepan and bring to a boil. Stir the cornstarch mixture into the liquid and continue cooking until the sauce has thickened, about 4 minutes. Add 1 teaspoon soy sauce, or to taste. Pour the sauce over the duck. Garnish with a few sprigs of cilantro.

Stuff again

PORK AND BEEF

Our family is versatile when it comes to cooking with meat, usually pork or beef. We stir-fry, deep-fry, roast, barbecue, and braise it, and we cook it in soups, with flavors ranging from sweet-and-sour to savory and the textures ranging from crisp to tender.

One pork dish we both love is *char siu,* glazed roasted pork. When we were five or six years old and visiting Annabel's father's restaurant, even before we entered Hong Kong Cafe, we could smell the aroma of *char siu* roasting. One cook would eye us, yell out, *"Mah mui!"*—Twins!—and threaten to knot our braids together permanently. Then he would look into our mortified faces, break into a grin, and instead slice off a bit of *char siu* for each of us. It was better than any candy.

A small quantity of meat is typically used as an ingredient in stir-frying. Less well known but just as delicious are homestyle or roasting recipes where seasonings are wonderfully blended with meat juices during long simmering. Slow-cooked meats are good dishes to make ahead because they provide variety to a multicourse Chinese meal without needing much last-minute attention. Also, for stews, hardened fat is easily removed from the sauce when it has been refriger-ated, and the meat is often even more flavorful the second day.

OLD CLAY POT

simple char siu

MAKES ABOUT 1¼ TO 1½ POUNDS

This version is made with a simpler marinade predominantly seasoned with hoisin sauce. It yields a sweeter result and is especially quick to put together.

1½–2 pounds boneless country-style
      pork spareribs
  ¼ cup honey

  ¼ cup hoisin sauce
  ¼ cup ketchup
  ½ teaspoon curing salt (see Note)

Cut the pork into strips about 6 inches long, 1 inch thick, and 1½ inches wide, if it isn't already cut that way when you purchase it. Odd-sized pieces are fine as long as they are about the same thickness so that they will cook in the same length of time.

In a bowl, mix together the honey, hoisin sauce, ketchup, and curing salt. Put the pork in a shallow pan large enough to hold the meat in one layer. Pour the seasoning mixture over the meat and turn the pieces to coat them evenly. Marinate for 3 hours in the refrigerator.

Heat the oven to 400°F. Place the meat on a rack over a roasting pan and cook for 20 to 30 minutes, or until the meat has cooked through. Test by removing a piece of meat from the oven and cutting through a thick portion. (Because the marinade has a lot of sugar in it, it will burn easily, so do not overcook.)

Cut diagonally into thin slices to serve as is or cool and use as directed in other recipes. Unsliced *char siu* may be wrapped and refrigerated for 2 or 3 days or frozen up to a month.

NOTE: Also known as saltpeter or sodium nitrate. If you omit this, the *char siu* will not take on its characteristic pink color and the texture will be closer to roast pork than ham, but the flavor will be much the same.

classic char siu

Char siu's crisp, sweet, and savory glaze and its moist succulent meat make it an attractive and popular dish. It is also very versatile and can be served thinly sliced as is, used as an ingredient in stir-fry dishes, added as a topping for soups, or used as the basis for *bao* filling.

1¹/₂–2 pounds boneless country-style pork spareribs	1 teaspoon fermented bean curd
1 garlic clove, finely chopped	4 teaspoons hoisin sauce
1 teaspoon salt	1 tablespoon ketchup
1¹/₂ teaspoons curing salt (see Note, page 136)	¹/₄ cup sugar
	2 tablespoons honey

Cut the pork into strips about 6 inches long, 1 inch thick, and 1¹/₂ inches wide, if it isn't already cut that way when you purchase it. Odd-sized pieces are fine as long as they are about the same thickness so that they will cook in the same length of time.

Combine the garlic, salt, curing salt, bean curd, hoisin sauce, ketchup, and sugar in a small bowl.

Put the pork in a shallow pan large enough to hold the meat in one layer. Pour the seasonings over the meat and turn the pieces to coat them evenly. Marinate for 3 hours in the refrigerator.

Heat the oven to 400°F. Place the meat on a rack over a roasting pan and cook for 20 to 30 minutes, or until the meat has cooked through. Test by removing a piece of meat from the oven and cutting through a thick portion. (Because the marinade has a lot of sugar in it, it will burn easily, so do not overcook.)

Remove from the oven. Brush the meat on both sides with the honey.

Cut diagonally into thin slices to serve as is or cool and use as directed in other recipes. Unsliced *char siu* may be wrapped and refrigerated for 2 or 3 days or frozen for up to a month.

Black Bean Spareribs

For this dish the ribs are chopped into tasty little 1-inch segments. Because this is a flavorful, easy, and economical dish, we had it quite often. It's even better the second day reheated 5 to 10 minutes in a steamer.

12 ounces to 1 pound pork spareribs

2 teaspoons cornstarch

1 tablespoon fermented black beans, rinsed and drained

3 dried hot chilies, seeded and crumbled (optional)

2 garlic cloves, finely chopped

1 tablespoon light soy sauce

1 teaspoon dry sherry or rice wine

½ teaspoon sugar

Cut the spareribs apart and chop into 1-inch lengths. Place in a bowl and toss with the cornstarch. Arrange the pieces to fit in a heatproof dish in one layer.

Combine the remaining ingredients in a bowl, then pour over the spareribs and marinate in the refrigerator for 1 hour.

Set a rack in a pot and add water to a depth of 1½ to 2 inches. (If you are using a steamer, fill the lower tier two-thirds full with water.) Bring to a boil. Set the steaming dish on the rack (or on the upper tier of a steamer) and steam until tender, about 30 to 40 minutes. After about 20 minutes, replenish the pot with boiling water if necessary. For less fat, make the spareribs a day ahead and refrigerate. Discard the hardened fat from the surface of the sauce before resteaming as above. Serve hot.

FERMENTED BLACK BEANS

DRIED HOT CHILIS

VARIATIONS

- ✦ **With Plum Sauce:** Substitute 1 teaspoon plum sauce for the sugar.
- ✦ **With Ginger:** Substitute ¾ teaspoon crushed garlic for the dried hot chilies.

Steamed Minced Pork Variations

MAKES 4 TO 6 SERVINGS

AS PART OF A CHINESE MEAL

DEEP
DISH

GLASS
PIE
PLATE

CAKE
PAN

When we asked our Chinese-American friends which homestyle recipes they remembered most fondly from childhood, steamed minced pork and its many variations was mentioned frequently. Although often served at home, it is rarely seen on a restaurant menu.

The best cuts of pork for this dish include the shoulder and boneless country-style ribs with some fat. Boneless pork chops are too lean and lack texture; when steamed, the meat will taste too dry. You may either grind the pork coarsely in a food processor or chop it with a cleaver. We remember some cooks in our family using a cleaver in each hand and chopping with a drumlike rhythm.

1 pound pork from the shoulder or boneless country-style ribs (not too lean)

1 teaspoon cornstarch mixed with 1 tablespoon cold water

Cut the pork into 1½-inch cubes. Place the pork in a food processor and pulse several times to grind coarsely; do not overgrind. Transfer to a bowl and mix in the cornstarch mixture and other ingredients. (See variations, pages 140–141.)

Instead of using a food processor, you may chop the pork with a Chinese cleaver. Add the other ingredients halfway through chopping, mixing in the cornstarch and water last.

Put the seasoned pork mixture into a heatproof dish and pat it into a 1-inch-thick patty. Set a rack in a pot and add water to a depth of 1½ to 2 inches. (If you are using a steamer, fill the lower tier half full with water.) Bring to a boil. Set the dish on the rack (or on the upper tier of a steamer) and steam for 40 to 45 minutes.

Use a turkey baster or spoon to discard some of the liquid that accumulates in the dish during steaming. Serve directly from the dish with a tablespoon in it so that diners may break off bits to serve themselves. Serve with rice.

WITH BLACK BEANS:

1   green onion, thinly sliced

1½ teaspoons fermented black beans, rinsed and drained

½   teaspoon salt

1   tablespoon dark soy sauce

Add all of the ingredients to the pork and pat the mixture into a heatproof dish. Steam as above.

WITH SALTED EGG:

1   salted preserved egg

1   green onion, very thinly sliced

1   fresh egg

PRESERVED
EGG

Omit the cornstarch mixture. Crack the salted preserved egg into a small bowl. Pick out the yolk, rinse it off under cold water, and set it aside. Reserve about 1 tablespoon of the white. The yolk should be firm and bright orange, and the egg should have a briny odor. If the yolk is soft and mustard-colored, and the white is gray or black and has a strong odor, the egg has spoiled and should be discarded.

Add the green onion and reserved egg white to the pork and proceed as directed above. Break the fresh egg into a small bowl and beat it lightly with a fork. Work it into the pork last. Pat the mixture into a heatproof dish.

With a small, sharp knife, cut the salted preserved egg yolk into 4 pieces. Flatten each piece with the side of a cleaver into a flat circle. Arrange the pieces evenly on top of the meat mixture and press them flat over the surface. Proceed as above.

WITH WATER CHESTNUTS:

6   fresh or canned water chestnuts, peeled if fresh, and finely minced

½   teaspoon salt

½   teaspoon sugar

½   teaspoon soy sauce

     Dash of pepper

1   tablespoon vegetable or peanut oil

Add the ingredients to the pork and proceed as above.

WATER CHESTNUTS

WITH DRIED SCALLOPS:

2–4 dried scallops

4 fresh or canned water chestnuts, peeled if fresh, and finely minced

½ teaspoon salt

½ teaspoon sugar

½ teaspoon soy sauce

Dash of pepper

1 tablespoon vegetable or peanut oil

DRIED SCALLOPS

Put the scallops in a small bowl and add just enough boiling water to cover. Let stand 30 minutes. Drain the scallops, reserving the soaking liquid, and shred them. Use 1 tablespoon of the reserved water to mix with the cornstarch as directed above. Add the remaining ingredients to the pork and proceed as above.

WITH SALTED FISH:

1 3 × 2-inch piece salted fish

1 green onion, thinly sliced

½ teaspoon salt

½ teaspoon soy sauce

Soak the salted fish in cold water for 15 minutes. Drain. Scrape off any remaining fish scales, then rinse and pat dry. Cut the fish into 4 pieces, each ¾ × 2 inches, and set aside.

Add the green onion, salt, and soy sauce to the pork. Put the mixture into a heatproof dish and pat into a 1-inch-thick patty. Arrange the fish on top of the pork and proceed as above.

WITH PRESERVED TURNIP:

1–1½ ounces chung choy (preserved turnip with greens attached)

1 teaspoon dry sherry or rice wine

Put the *chung choy* in a small bowl with water to cover for 4 hours or overnight. You can use any combination of the *chung choy* root or greens. Rinse and finely mince the *chung choy*. Add to the pork with the sherry and proceed as above.

PRESERVED TURNIP

Sweet-and-Sour Pork

MAKES 4 TO 6 SERVINGS AS PART OF A CHINESE MEAL

Sweet mixed Chinese pickles contribute a crunchy texture and the bite of sweetened ginger to deep-fried cubes of pork. Two chicken variations follow, including a leaner pan-fried version.

SAUCE

- ¼ cup water
- ¼ cup cider vinegar
- ½ cup firmly packed brown sugar
- 2 tablespoons ketchup
- 1 tablespoon cornstarch mixed with 3 tablespoons water

- 2 teaspoons sesame seeds (optional), for garnish

2–3 cups peanut oil for deep-frying

- 1 pound pork from the shoulder or boneless country-style ribs (not too lean), cut into 1-inch cubes
- 2 tablespoons cornstarch

- 1 tablespoon vegetable or peanut oil for the wok
- 1 bell pepper, cored, seeded, and cut into 1-inch squares
- ½ medium red or yellow onion, quartered and separated into layers
- ¼ fresh pineapple, cored and cut into 1-inch chunks, or 1 cup canned chunks, drained
- 1 11-ounce can lychees (optional)
- ⅔ cup mixed Chinese pickles, drained (optional)
- 6–8 Chinese pickled shallots, drained (optional)

To make the sauce, combine the water, vinegar, brown sugar, and ketchup in a small enamel saucepan. Cook over low heat, stirring occasionally, until the sugar has dissolved, 3 to 4 minutes. Stir in the cornstarch mixture, bring to a boil, and cook 2 to 3 minutes over medium-low heat, until the sauce is thick and translucent. Remove from the heat and keep warm.

Place a nonstick skillet over medium heat, add the sesame seeds, if using, to the dry skillet, and toast them until they are lightly browned, about 2 minutes, shaking the pan gently. Remove the sesame seeds immediately to cool; leaving them in the hot skillet may cause them to burn. Set aside.

Line a cookie sheet with several layers of paper towels and set aside.

Heat the oil to 360°F. in a deep skillet or wok. Dredge the pork in the cornstarch, then divide it into 3 batches. Put the pieces from the first batch one at a time into the oil. Cook 4 to 5 minutes, until browned, turning to brown evenly. Cut through one piece to test for doneness; it should be white and opaque throughout. Remove the pork with a slotted spoon and let it drain on the prepared cookie sheet while you cook the remaining batches.

Place a nonaluminum pan or nonstick wok over medium heat, then heat 1 tablespoon oil. Add the pepper and onion and stir-fry until the onion is wilted and transparent, 4 to 5 minutes. Add the pork, pineapple, and the lychees, mixed pickles, and shallots, if using, and continue cooking until heated through, about 2 to 3 minutes. Add the sauce and cook about 1 minute longer. Place in a serving bowl and sprinkle the sesame seeds on top.

VARIATIONS

◆ **Sweet-and-Sour Chicken:** Substitute 1 pound skinless, boneless chicken for the pork. Cut the chicken into 1-inch cubes and proceed as above. (Dark meat will take slightly longer to cook than light meat.)

◆ **Sweet-and-Sour Pan-Fried Chicken:** For a leaner version, substitute 1 whole chicken breast for the pork. Run your thumb between the tenders and outer chicken breast to partially detach them. Lay the breast open with the tenders out to the side. Pat the chicken dry and dredge in cornstarch.

Instead of deep-frying, heat 1 tablespoon oil in a nonstick skillet. Add the chicken and brown on both sides, about 7 minutes on each side. (Cut through the thickest part to test for doneness.) Let it cool slightly, then cut into 1-inch cubes. Proceed as above.

◆ **Orange-Flavored Sweet-and-Sour Sauce:** Stir ½ teaspoon grated orange rind and 1 tablespoon orange juice into the sauce just before removing it from the heat.

Pork Loin Roast

We usually served this hearty pork roast American style, with rice and a vegetable, rather than as one of many courses in a Chinese meal. Red bean curd gives this pork roast a Chinese twist.

- 1 boneless pork loin roast, about 3½ to 4 pounds
- 1 teaspoon salt
- ¼ teaspoon pepper
- ½ teaspoon sugar
- 2 tablespoons soy sauce
- ½ teaspoon dry sherry or rice wine
- 1 tablespoon water
- 1 tablespoon red bean curd
- 1 tablespoon cornstarch mixed with ¼ cup water or chicken broth

RED BEAN CURD

Rub the pork loin with the salt and pepper. In a small bowl, mix together the sugar, soy sauce, dry sherry, water, and red bean curd. Rub the mixture over the meat. Preheat the oven to 350°F. Place the meat directly into a shallow roasting pan, not on a rack, and insert a meat thermometer into the thickest part. Roast for 30 minutes, then add 1 cup hot water to the pan. After another 45 minutes, add ½ cup hot water. Roast until the thermometer reaches 180°F., about 1½ to 1¾ hours total, depending on the size of the roast.

Remove the meat from the pan and keep it warm. Pour the pan juices through a sieve into a saucepan, scraping up any brown bits. Skim off as much fat as possible. Add about ¾ cup water to the saucepan. Taste and add more water if it seems too salty. Bring it just to a boil, then stir in the cornstarch mixture and continue cooking until the sauce has thickened, about 5 minutes.

Cut the meat into ½-inch-thick slices and arrange them on a warm serving platter. Spoon a little sauce over the meat and serve the remaining sauce separately.

Roast Beef

This was our family's version of an American staple. To serve such large portions of meat as a main course was unusual in traditional Chinese cooking.

MARINADE
1 garlic clove, chopped
1 tablespoon chopped fresh ginger
2 tablespoons light soy sauce
1 tablespoon dry sherry or rice wine
⅛ teaspoon sugar

4–6 pounds cross-rib roast
Salt and pepper
1 teaspoon oyster sauce, or to taste (optional)
2½ teaspoons cornstarch mixed with ¼ cup cold water

Set a rack in a shallow roasting pan. Pour about 3 cups water into the pan to just below the level of the rack.

Combine the garlic and ginger with the soy sauce, dry sherry, and sugar in a small bowl. Place the meat on the rack and sprinkle all over with salt and pepper. Rub the marinade all over the meat, letting the excess drip into the roasting pan. Let stand for 30 minutes.

Preheat the oven to 350° F. Insert a meat thermometer into the thickest part of the meat and roast approximately 20 to 25 minutes per pound, or until the meat thermometer reaches 140° F. for rare, 160° F. for medium, or 170° F. for well done. Add about 1 cup water to the roasting pan about halfway through the cooking time to just below the original water level in the pan.

Remove the roast from the rack and let it rest 15 minutes in a warm place while you make the gravy. Strain the pan juices through a sieve into a saucepan. Skim off as much fat as possible. (Defatted, you should have about 2 cups.) Bring the gravy to a boil. Add oyster sauce to taste, if desired. Lower the heat and stir in the cornstarch mixture. Continue cooking until the sauce has thickened, about 5 minutes.

Slice the roast to the desired thickness and serve with the gravy on the side.

Barbecued Flank Steak on Skewers

MAKES 25 TO 30 SKEWERS (ALLOW 2 TO 3 PER PERSON)

Fourth of July was a joyous holiday for our family. We usually celebrated at Ellen's family's farm. The women cooked garlic fried chicken, potato salad, barbecued spareribs, barbecued flank steak on skewers, chow mein, shrimp dumplings, and other food, while the men set up Red Devil fireworks for the evening display.

After we ate, we sat outside to watch the fireworks. The smell of alfalfa fields filled the summer night air as we watched the stars and sparklers glow. We thought how lucky we were to be Americans—to be free and safe and well fed.

30	8- to 10-inch bamboo skewers
2	pounds flank steak
1	1-inch piece ginger, peeled, sliced, and crushed
2	green onions, thinly sliced
1	garlic clove, minced
3	tablespoons red wine vinegar
2	teaspoons cornstarch
1	teaspoon salt
½	cup water
1½	teaspoons sugar
¼	teaspoon baking soda
2	tablespoons soy sauce
¼	cup peanut oil
4	teaspoons oyster sauce
	Dash of pepper

Soak the bamboo skewers in hot water for at least 1 hour. This will prevent them from burning.

Cut the flank steak diagonally into very thin 1 × 2-inch slices. (This is easier if you freeze the meat for about 30 minutes, until firm but not frozen hard, just before cutting it.)

Mix the ginger, green onions, and garlic with the remaining ingredients in a large bowl. Add the meat and marinate for 1 hour. (Do not marinate longer because the baking soda will change the texture of the meat.)

Prepare a charcoal fire 30 to 45 minutes before grilling, depending on the type of charcoal you use. The barbecue is ready when the charcoal is covered with a layer of white ash. Spray the grill with a vegetable oil cooking spray before putting it in place.

Thread 3 or 4 slices of meat on each skewer. Grill 2 or 3 minutes on each side, checking for doneness after about 5 minutes total. Grill longer if necessary, but watch the meat carefully, as it cooks very quickly.

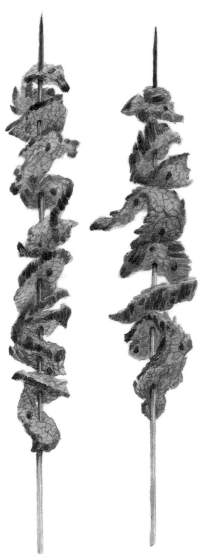

The Importance of Food

ELLEN

As a girl in China, my mother and the rest of the women ate only after the men had finished. Most days, dinner consisted of rice and vegetables accompanied by a bit of salted fish. My uncle ate better and sometimes had the additional treat of a spoonful of lard stirred into his rice.

Our relatives here lived vastly better than our relatives in China. Everyone had electricity, a refrigerator, a modern stove, and indoor plumbing. By American standards, we were not well off, but not once did we go hungry. Food meant we were wealthy. Food meant we were secure.

We did not spend extravagantly on food. We shopped for food on sale. We grew what we could. Inexpensive cuts and organ meats regularly appeared on the table—tripe, liver, kidneys, tongue, oxtail, and a few parts I still can't identify. When I was five or six, my favorite food was not candy, but chicken feet, salvaged from my grandfather's restaurant and stewed in a rich tomato broth. We children soon learned that we could astonish our friends at school by relating what we had enjoyed for dinner the night before.

Many of our family photographs catch someone, somewhere, chewing. Much family energy was spent arguing the merits of this vegetable or that fish. Food offered a way for my parents to communicate their love for us when words failed. It became a passion we could all share and we took our family's preoccupation with food for granted. What a surprise to find out as an adult that not everyone shared our outlook. One way I know I'm still Chinese is because of my attitude toward food.

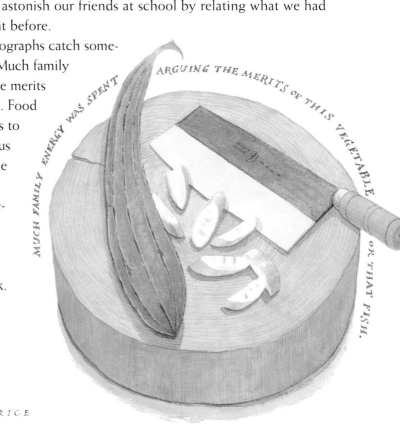

MUCH FAMILY ENERGY WAS SPENT ARGUING THE MERITS OF THIS VEGETABLE OR THAT FISH.

Beef Tongue

Beef tongue has a more tender texture than beef stew meat, and it's even better made a day in advance. Cut into slices and reheat just before serving.

1 beef tongue, about 3 to 3½ pounds	½ teaspoon brown bean sauce
1 tablespoon vegetable or peanut oil	2 teaspoons red bean curd
1–2 garlic cloves, finely chopped	1 whole star anise
1 teaspoon minced fresh ginger	1 teaspoon dry sherry or rice wine
½ onion, thinly sliced	1 tablespoon soy sauce
½ teaspoon salt	1 tablespoon cornstarch mixed with
Dash of pepper	¼ cup water

Rinse the tongue well. Fill a large pot two-thirds full with water and bring to a boil. Add the tongue and simmer 1 hour, until the outer layer of the tongue turns opaque white.

Drain the tongue and let it cool for 10 minutes. Place it on a cutting board, trim off and discard the outer layer, and halve the tongue lengthwise.

Place a wok over high heat and heat the oil. Add the tongue and brown it on all sides, 7 to 10 minutes. Add the garlic, ginger, onion, salt, and pepper. Lower the heat if the oil begins to smoke.

When the tongue is brown and the onion is translucent, 7 to 8 minutes, add the brown bean sauce, red bean curd, star anise, dry sherry, and soy sauce with about 3 cups water, or enough to almost cover the tongue.

Lower the heat, cover, and simmer for 2½ hours, until the tongue feels tender when pierced with a fork.

Remove the tongue from the sauce and allow it to cool slightly. Strain the sauce through a sieve. Reheat the sauce to a boil, stir in the cornstarch mixture, and continue cooking until the sauce has thickened, about 5 minutes.

Slice the tongue crosswise into ½-inch-thick slices and reheat in the sauce.

Stewed Short Ribs

Hearty, meaty short ribs are especially succulent when braised in a flavorful broth accented with tangerine peel and star anise. The spices blend and mellow over the slow cooking and the dish is even better if made a day ahead. See the variations below if you prefer to make oxtail stew or leaner beef stew.

2½–3 pounds beef short ribs

2 teaspoons vegetable or peanut oil

1 tablespoon red bean curd

1 1-inch piece ginger, peeled and thinly sliced

1 yellow onion, halved and then quartered and separated into layers

3–4 whole star anise

1 tablespoon soy sauce

1 teaspoon dry sherry or rice wine

Pinch of Chinese five-spice powder

1 1 × ¾-inch piece tangerine peel (see Glossary) (optional)

1 green bell pepper, seeds removed, cut into 1½-inch squares

2½ teaspoons cornstarch mixed with ¼ cup water

Oyster sauce (optional)

Have the butcher cut the short ribs into 2-inch lengths. Rinse and pat dry.

Place a wok or heavy Dutch oven over medium-high heat. Heat the oil. Add the red bean curd, ginger, onion, and short ribs. Brown the meat on all sides, about 15 minutes. Add the star anise, soy sauce, dry sherry, five-spice powder, tangerine peel, if using, and enough water to almost cover the meat (about 2 to 3 cups).

Lower the heat and simmer, covered, until the meat is tender, about 2 to 2½ hours. About 10 minutes before the meat is done, scatter the peppers over the top and continue to cook, covered. Skim off and discard as much fat as possible from the sauce.

Stir in the cornstarch mixture and continue cooking until the sauce has thickened, about 5 minutes. Add 1 tablespoon oyster sauce, or to taste, and serve.

VARIATIONS

✦ **Oxtail Stew:** Substitute 3½ pounds oxtails for the short ribs and chicken broth for some or all of the water. Skim off any fat or foam that rises to the surface. Replenish the pot with water or chicken broth as necessary. Simmer the oxtails until tender, about 4 hours. Omit the bell pepper and add 2 carrots, peeled and cut into 1-inch slices, about 20 minutes before the oxtails are done.

✦ **Beef Stew:** Substitute 1½ pounds lean beef stew cut into 1½-inch cubes for the short ribs and proceed as above.

OXTAIL STEW VARIATION

While my father lived at his sister's farm, single Chinese men were often hired as farm-workers. As partial compensation, the workers were given three meals every day, rain or shine, prepared in a special cookhouse built to feed twenty to fifty men at a time.

My father was inspired to refine his construction skills by building in some woks for the cookhouse. Three woks, each about a yard in diameter, were positioned over holes in a cement slab. The brick supporting structure was interlaced with gas lines and burners, and a faucet was positioned high over each wok so that the woks could be easily filled or washed. The back of the cement slab was indented with a trough, with a drain hole at one end, so that after the woks were scrubbed, the dirty water could be sloshed out into the trough and drained.

In contrast, few other kitchens in the family were large or well appointed. Some were so small that two people could hardly maneuver around each other without touching. Electric frying pans and deep fryers were set on washing machines on back porches or in garages for lack of other space. Old refrigerators and deep freezers shared garage space with cars; one especially fine commercial refrigerator resided in a bedroom.

Kitchen walls were glazed with layers of vaporized oil. Tins, thermoses full of hot tea, and breadboxes vied for room on scant counterspace. The pungent odor of salted fish mingled with the earthy smell of black mushrooms soaking in hot water and

MISMATCHED PLATES STACKED HIGH WHEREVER THERE WAS ROOM.

green onions fresh from the garden waiting to be washed. A pork leg simmering all day in a rich broth contributed its fragrant steam.

Drawers held worn cleavers of different weights for vegetables or meats. Large dented aluminum steaming pots took up whole lower shelves. Well-seasoned woks sat permanently on stovetops. Small appliances were packed into closets and under beds. Extra mismatched plates, bowls, platters, and cups nested together in precariously high stacks, piled anywhere there was room.

Knee-high tins that once held lard at my grandfather's restaurant served as makeshift storage containers. Our closet floors were lined with tins filled with flour, dried fruit, and rice, originally purchased in fifty- or hundred-pound sacks. In the hall closet, shelves were laden with musky winter melons larger than basketballs. Elsewhere shelves were jammed with canned and dried food from our semiannual grocery shopping trips to San Francisco's Chinatown. Overflows of supplies were stashed under our high Victorian beds, sharing space with folding chairs.

And yet, even with such facilities, miracles happened.

Oyster Beef with Broccoli

No Chinese cookbook seems complete without a recipe for oyster beef. There are many versions; sometimes it is even served over rice with a fried egg on top. This is a versatile dish because the beef may be combined with whatever vegetables you have on hand if broccoli is not available.

1 *pound flank steak*

1 *pound broccoli*

MARINADE

1 teaspoon oyster sauce

2 teaspoons soy sauce

1½ teaspoons rice wine or dry sherry

⅛ teaspoon sugar

Dash of white pepper

½ teaspoon sesame oil

1½ teaspoons cornstarch

SAUCE

3 tablespoons oyster sauce

½ cup chicken broth

½ teaspoon soy sauce

1 tablespoon cornstarch

1 tablespoon vegetable or peanut oil

Cut the flank steak diagonally into very thin 1 × 2-inch slices. (This is easier if you freeze the meat about 30 minutes, until firm but not frozen hard, just before cutting it.)

Combine the marinade ingredients in a medium bowl. Add the flank steak and mix to coat the meat well. Marinate for 30 minutes.

Cut the broccoli crosswise about 4 inches below the flower head. Separate the florets into manageable-sized pieces. With a paring knife, peel and cut the stem part into ½ × ½-inch pieces.

In a large saucepan, bring 8 cups water to a boil. Add the broccoli and cook about 3 minutes, until it is crisp-tender but still bright green. Drain the broccoli in a colander.

In a small bowl, mix together the oyster sauce, chicken broth, soy sauce, and cornstarch and set aside.

Place a wok over high heat and heat the oil. Add the flank steak and stir-fry until browned on the outside but still somewhat pink in the middle, about 3 minutes. Add the broccoli and cook 30 seconds to 1 minute longer, until heated through. Add the sauce ingredients and cook until the sauce has thickened, about 1 minute. Serve immediately.

VARIATION

Ginger Beef: Peel and crush 1 garlic clove, or mince it finely. Peel a 1-inch piece of ginger and cut it into thin slivers. After heating the oil in the wok, add the garlic and ginger and stir-fry 30 seconds before adding the beef. Proceed as above.

Steamed Sliced Beef

When you want something uncomplicated, this dish fits the bill. When beef is steamed, it releases its true flavor, making its own fragrant broth. A few spoonfuls of the broth over steamed rice adds a nice homey touch.

1	pound beef flank steak or sirloin	¼	teaspoon sugar
1	tablespoon soy sauce	½	teaspoon cornstarch
2	teaspoons dry sherry or rice wine	¼	teaspoon sesame oil
½	teaspoon salt	1	green onion, thinly sliced

Cut the beef across the grain into thin strips approximately ⅛ × ⅛ × 1½ inches. (This is easier if you freeze the meat for about 30 minutes, until firm but not frozen hard, just before cutting it.)

In a heatproof dish, combine the soy sauce, dry sherry, salt, sugar, cornstarch, sesame oil, and green onion. Add the beef and mix well.

Set a rack in a pot and add water to a depth of 1½ to 2 inches. (If you are using a steamer, fill the lower tier half full with water.) Bring to a boil. Set the dish on the rack (or upper tier of a steamer) and steam over high heat for 15 minutes. Serve directly from the steaming dish with a large spoon in it so diners may serve themselves.

BEARING GIFTS: HOLIDAYS AND FAMILY CELEBRATIONS

Our family's close ties were reinforced by gatherings to mark celebrations and holidays, both large and small. Relatives and Chinese friends never arrived empty-handed, but always bore edible gifts.

Depending on what Chinese village a person came from, however, the same gift could be perceived as a symbol of good luck—or as an insult. For example, bananas and peanuts, symbols of fertility, were a common gift in our family. To someone from another village, however, peanuts symbolized bodies inside coffins.

Food was not given in multiples of four because four, or *see*, sounds like the word for death. Even now, only Americanized dim sum restaurants serve four tidbits to a plate instead of the more awkward three. If the gift were to be American pastry, doughnuts might be avoided because all one's luck could run out the hole in the middle.

Anything that symbolizes cutting life short is not an acceptable birthday gift. Therefore, if one forgetfully makes a gift of a fine knife or scissors, the recipient is likely to press a *lee see* envelope with a dollar bill inside as symbolic "payment" for them so that the giver is blameless for any harm the blade may cause in the future.

On their birthdays, we honored our elders by presenting them with cups of tea, sweetened with a dried jujube and a slice of candied lotus root. Holding the teacup in both hands, we were instructed to say, "Honored relation, drink tea." We children lined up balancing teacups on overheated fingers as the honoree patiently took a sip from each cup as if it were the only one. As we honored the elders, they in turn made us feel special and important by thanking us with a *lee see* envelope.

chinese New Year

Eager anticipation always preceded New Year's Day. We were assigned to polish furniture, wax floors, shine pots, and scrub everything. A special New Year's cake steamed on the stove all day, filling the house with its sweetness. Pyramids of pomelos (Chinese grapefruit) and tangerines balanced on the dining table and atop the television. Red *lee see* envelopes filled with good luck coins were tucked into the rice tin and displayed next to the wok as an offering to the kitchen god.

We started New Year's morning by tearing open our own *lee see*, which our parents slipped under a pair of tangerines at our bedsides as we slept. The envelopes usually contained only a few coins, but it began our next days' collection of *lee see* from all married relatives, and most of those contained crisp dollar bills. We were taught to pretend to refuse the envelopes, but it was understood by all that we were to keep the money.

Tradition prevailed at our New Year's breakfast of steamed rice, boiled lettuce, and *jeh*, a vegetarian monks' dish full of ingredients symbolizing good luck and prosperity. As we got older, we tried to show how sophisticated we were by proclaiming loudly that we'd much prefer our American breakfast of eggs, bacon, and toast, but on this day at least, the new ways gave way to the old.

All day we dined on foods chosen because their names sound like words associated with good fortune and wealth or because they resembled money. Oysters, *hoh see*, sound like luck; fish, *ngee*, sounds like the word for abundance; lily buds, *gum jem*, or "golden needles," symbolize gold. Lettuce, *song choy*, sounds like growing luck and looks like green paper money. Tossed with oyster sauce, it is doubly lucky. Long-grain rice symbolizes a long life. Sweet dishes predict a sweet life.

Some dishes were presented at the table whole to symbolize the wholeness and fullness of life. Preparing a whole fried fish for New Year's dinner was always an anxious time. Breaking the wholeness of the delicate fish while preparing it portended bad luck for the year. We watched nervously as the fish was turned over slowly and gently so as not to break the tail. Sometimes it worked and we cheered, and sometimes it didn't. No matter. When it didn't work, our practical natures prevailed. We simply held the tail together with a toothpick and flipped the fish over to show the good side.

We weren't to sweep or empty the trash on New Year's, since we might inadvertently throw out our luck. We weren't to cry, because it would bring a sad year. We weren't to wash our luck away by washing our hair. For us children, New Year's meant our parents were not supposed to yell at us lest discord follow throughout the year. It amused us to watch our parents try to control their tempers and to speak pleasantly no matter what we did.

For two or three days following New Year's, relatives paid visits back and forth until everyone had been to everyone else's home to exchange slabs of New Year's cake and wishes for happiness and prosperity.

New Year's was also a procrastinator's delight. If resolutions got broken after January 1, we could always start over at Chinese New Year about a month later. The new year still never feels like it has begun until after Chinese New Year.

POMELOS and TANGERINES decorate tables for NEW YEAR'S DAY

chinese New Year's cake

In China, New Year's cakes were made in bamboo steamers two feet across and a foot high. The strenuous task of working large quantities of batter was one of the few cooking assignments given to the men in the family. Large, pliable banana leaves lined the steamers to keep batter from over-flowing the sides as the cake expanded during cooking. A full day of steaming was required to cook the cakes thoroughly. This version is much easier.

Don't expect a light cake full of air pockets. This chewy cake, lightly sweetened with yams and Chinese brown sugar, is more like a soft caramel. We never did this, but in some villages, ½ cup Chinese sausage or pork fat cut in ¼-inch dice is kneaded into the batter.

The cake can be made 1 to 3 days in advance and should be refrigerated after the first or second day. Leftover cake may be cut into ½-inch-thick slices, dipped in beaten eggs, fried until browned over medium heat in an oiled nonstick skillet 1 to 2 minutes on each side, and served with maple syrup. The cake will be slightly crisp on the outside and chewy inside.

1	pound Chinese brown sugar bars	1⅓	cups mashed cooked or canned yams
1¾	cups water	1	jujube, for garnish (optional)
1½	teaspoons vegetable or peanut oil	¼	teaspoon sesame seeds, for garnish
4¾	cups glutinous rice flour		(optional)

In a small saucepan, bring the sugar and water to a boil. Lower the heat and simmer 6 or 7 minutes, until the sugar has dissolved. Set aside to cool until it is
barely warm. When cooled, mix in the oil and reserve ¼ cup of the syrup.

In a large bowl, combine the flour and yams. Add the remaining syrup and mix
in with your hands, lifting the batter between your fingers and squeezing it back
into the bowl. The batter becomes very sticky and thick; working it requires a lot
of effort. Work the batter at least 10 minutes; the longer it is worked, the better
and chewier the cake will be.

Generously oil a 9-inch round cake pan or a 1½- to 2-quart heatproof bowl.
(A bowl with straight sides such as a soufflé dish works best.) Pour the batter into
the pan, wet your hands, and pat the top smooth. Rap the pan sharply against the
countertop to force air bubbles to rise to the top. Break the bubbles with your fingertips and smooth over. Spread the reserved syrup over the top.

Set a rack in a pot and add water to a depth of 2 inches. (If you are using a
steamer add water to the lower tier until almost full.) Bring to a boil. Lower the
pan onto the rack (or put on the upper tier of a steamer). Steam the cake over
high heat for 4 hours, replenishing the pot with boiling water every 20 to 30 minutes as the water in the pot evaporates. You may want to add the water through a
large metal funnel because the water must not splash onto the cake.

If you like, about 5 minutes before the cake is done, you can put a jujube in
the middle of the top of the cake (for luck) and/or sprinkle with sesame seeds.

Remove the cake from the pot or steamer, let the cake cool to room temperature, cover it with foil, and let it rest overnight. (Refrigerate it if you are making it
more than 1 day ahead. Reheat it by steaming 10 minutes, then let it cool again
to room temperature unless you like a very soft, sticky cake.) Turn the cake out
onto a serving plate and cut it into ¼-inch-thick slices.

NOTE: The recipe may be doubled. You may have to add a little extra rice flour to
the batter because you do not double the amount of syrup reserved for the top of
the cake. Steam the cake in an oiled 4½-quart heatproof bowl for 6 to 7 hours.

This cake freezes well. Let it thaw, then steam 20 to 30 minutes, depending on
the size of the cake section. You may also cut thawed cake into 1-inch slices and
microwave it, covered, on medium heat for 1 minute.

vegetarian Monks' Dish (Jeh)

Every ingredient in this traditional Chinese New Year breakfast symbolizes something good for the new year—luck, prosperity, or good fortune. *Hoh see*, oyster, is a homonym for good fortune, explaining its presence in this vegetarian dish. Although soaking the individual ingredients takes time, most of the steps may be done one day ahead. Besides, it's worth a little effort to begin the new year with a multitude of good omens.

1	3½-ounce package bean threads
20	small dried black mushrooms
½	ounce cloud ears
½	cup tiger lily buds
20	small dried jujubes (Chinese red dates)
½	ounce fat choy (black seaweed)
¼	cup dried lotus seeds
½	teaspoon salt
1	teaspoon plus 1 tablespoon vegetable or peanut oil
1	½-inch piece ginger
8–12	dried oysters, soaked overnight in water to cover (optional)
¾	cup shelled ginkgo nuts
2	ounces dried bean curd sticks (also called dried bean flour skins)
4	ounces snow peas, strings removed

SEASONING MIXTURE

3	cups water
1	tablespoon sugar
4	teaspoons oyster sauce
1	tablespoon soy sauce

8–10	ounces tofu, cut into ¾-inch dice
8	fresh or canned water chestnuts, peeled and sliced
¼	cup sliced bamboo shoots, rinsed and drained
4–8	fresh arrowheads, lightly scraped but with stems intact
12	pieces dao pok (fried wheat gluten)
2	cups finely shredded napa cabbage
1	tablespoon red bean curd
1	tablespoon fermented bean curd Steamed Rice (page 35)
1–2	cubes each fermented and red bean curd, in separate small dishes

TIGER
LILY
BUDS

WATER
CHESTNUT

NAPA
CABBAGE

BEAN
THREADS

FAT CHOY
SEAWEED

DAO POK
(Fried
Wheat
Gluten)

SNOW PEA

CLOUD
EARS

BAMBOO
SHOOTS

LOTUS
SEEDS

BEAN CURD
STICK

JUJUBE
(Chinese
Red Date)

GINKGO
NUT

ARROW~
HEAD

BLACK
MUSHROOM

TOFU

Soak the bean threads in water to cover for 2 hours. Meanwhile, put the mushrooms in a small bowl with hot water to cover. Let stand 30 to 45 minutes to soften. Cut off and discard the hard stems. Rinse the caps, squeeze them dry, and cut into ¼-inch-thick slices.

Put the cloud ears, tiger lily buds, jujubes, *fat choy*, and lotus seeds in separate bowls, add hot water to cover, and soak for 30 minutes.

Rinse the cloud ears well, drain, then cut off and discard any hard parts. Rinse and drain the tiger lily buds, then cut off the hard ends. Drain the jujubes.

Rinse the *fat choy* and put it in a small saucepan with the salt, 1 teaspoon of the oil, the ginger, and water to cover. Bring to a boil, turn off the heat, and let stand 10 minutes. Drain the *fat choy* then gently squeeze out the water.

Open the lotus seeds and discard the bitter green part inside. Put the lotus seeds in a small saucepan with water to cover, bring to a boil, then lower the heat and simmer until tender, about 20 minutes. Drain.

Rinse the soaked oysters to remove any sand. Trim off any tough parts, then steam the oysters in a small dish for 10 minutes over medium heat until soft.

Put the ginkgo nuts in a small saucepan with enough water to cover. Bring to a boil, lower the heat, and simmer 5 minutes. Drain, then skin.

Break the bean curd sticks into 2- to 3-inch pieces. Soak for 30 minutes in a small saucepan with water to cover, simmer about 10 minutes to soften, then drain.

Drain the bean threads, then cut into 6-inch lengths.

You can prepare the recipe to this point one day in advance. Cover the individual ingredients separately and refrigerate.

Blanch the snow peas in boiling water for 30 seconds, then rinse them under cold water and drain.

Combine the seasoning mixture ingredients in a medium bowl and set aside.

Combine the mushrooms, cloud ears, tiger lily buds, *fat choy*, lotus seeds, oysters, ginkgo nuts, tofu, water chestnuts, bamboo shoots, arrowheads, and *dao pok* in a large bowl. Combine the bean threads and bean curd sticks in a second bowl, and the jujubes, cabbage, and snow peas in a third bowl.

Heat a wok over high heat, then heat 1 tablespoon oil. Add the red and fermented bean curd, lower the heat to medium-high, and cook 15 seconds, breaking it up with a spatula. Stir in the seasoning mixture, bring to a boil, and boil for 2 to 3 minutes. Add the mushroom mixture and cook for 10 minutes, stirring occasionally.

Add the bean threads and bean curd sticks and cook 4 minutes longer, stirring occasionally. Add the remaining ingredients and cook 2 minutes longer, tossing gently to distribute the cabbage evenly.

Serve with the rice and small dishes of red and fermented bean curd.

New Baby

ANNABEL

A JADE HEART

calms the heart

Once my older sister complained to Father that she couldn't keep her house neat however hard she tried. Father comforted her with a bit of his philosophy. "A messy house is a happy house because it means children live there."

My parents loved children. The top of the sideboard in one room was stacked five deep with photographs of children and grandchildren at every age. In one snapshot, Father proudly showed off an infant grandson in each arm. ·

In the old days in China, a family would dare to celebrate only if a baby survived its precarious first month. Although times have changed, many Chinese families still wait until baby's first month passes to give a party.

Every time a baby turned a month old in our family, there was great excitement. Older relatives crowded around the new mother and baby, shouting conflicting advice and vying greedily to wrest the baby from her arms for a turn to coo, cajole, and jostle it ever more violently until it either finally smiled or wailed in protest. Guests would study the baby and bluntly predict the baby's character based on its features. Long earlobes meant long life, while small earlobes meant intelligence. Big eyes indicated alertness. Small hands predicted wealth. A small rosebud mouth foretold eloquence.

Meanwhile, Mother helped prepare traditional food for the parties. The dining table was bright with red-dyed hard-cooked eggs, symbolizing fertility, and a dish of pickled carrots, radish, and ginger. The women tended pots of simmering vinegary pigs' feet and a special chicken soup laced with whiskey. And they kept an eye open for the occasional mischievous child who tried to sneak a forbidden spoonful.

Guests tucked red *lee see*, envelopes filled with money, into the baby's blanket. Close relatives gave the baby small gold bracelets or rings, tiny jade bangle bracelets, or jade carved into pendants shaped like hearts or peaches for girls or fish or miniature Buddhas for boys. The newest family member had been initiated.

whiskey chicken

MAKES 6 TO 8 SERVINGS

As far as we can remember, this dish has always been served to guests visiting a new mother and baby. The new mother should probably only indulge in a small taste, however, as the spirits are quite potent. To reduce the alcohol content, increase the water to 6 cups or substitute milder rice wine for the whiskey.

12 small dried black mushrooms	1 2-inch piece ginger, peeled and cut into 4 or 5 slices
24 tiger lily buds	1 teaspoon salt
1 ounce dried wood ears	3 cups water
1 3½- to 4½-pound chicken	3 cups Sam Ching Chinese distilled spirits
8–12 jujubes (Chinese red dates)	
½ cup raw peanuts	

Put the mushrooms in a small bowl with hot water to cover. Let stand 30 to 45 minutes to soften. Cut off and discard the hard stems. Rinse the caps and squeeze them dry. Cut the larger mushrooms in half.

Put the tiger lily buds in a small bowl and cover with hot water. Let stand 30 minutes to soften. Cut off and discard the hard stem ends.

Put the wood ears in a medium bowl and cover with hot water. Let stand 30 minutes to soften. Cut off and discard any hard parts. Cut the larger pieces into about 1-inch pieces.

Cut the chicken into pieces small enough to be eaten with chopsticks. Cut the thighs and drumsticks in half, separate the wing parts, and cut each breast crosswise into 3 or 4 pieces.

Place all the ingredients in a large stockpot and bring to a boil over high heat. Lower the heat and simmer for 1 hour, until the chicken is tender, skimming off any fat or foam.

Serve the chicken in small bowls, with a little of the broth.

NOTE: For a leaner version, skin the chicken before cooking it.

Pickled Pigs' Feet with Ginger

MAKES 4 TO 6 SERVINGS

Old relatives advised a new mother to chew the ginger from this dish, then blow warm gingery breath on her new baby's head and rub the head gently to encourage a round shape. As children, we watched dubiously, awaiting the instant transformation of the new baby's head.

Well-wishers coming to see a new baby were always treated to bowlfuls of steaming pickled pigs' feet. This is best when made one or two days ahead.

2–4 pigs' feet, split and cut into 2-inch lengths (3½–4 pounds)

½ teaspoon salt

1 tablespoon brown sugar

5 cups Chinese black vinegar

¼ pound ginger, peeled and cut into 1-inch chunks

1¼ cups dark brown sugar

6–8 eggs, hard-cooked, in their shells (optional)

Bring 4 quarts of water to a boil in a large enamel pot. (Do not use an aluminum pot.) Add the pigs' feet, salt, and 1 tablespoon brown sugar. Bring the water back to a boil and boil 30 minutes. Drain and rinse the pigs' feet in a colander under cold water. Remove any hair or discoloration with a paring knife. Wash the pot.

Bring the vinegar to a boil in the same pot. Add the pigs' feet, lower the heat, and simmer, covered, for 10 minutes. Add the ginger and dark brown sugar and continue to simmer, covered, for 45 to 50 minutes, or until tender. Add the eggs, if using, during the last 30 minutes of cooking.

Allow the pigs' feet to cool in the pot, then cover and refrigerate overnight to let the flavors mellow.

To serve, discard the hardened fat from the surface of the vinegar and reheat. Spoon the pigs' feet into individual bowls with a little of the vinegar and some ginger. Peel the eggs and add them on top or serve them separately.

Ching Ming

ANNABEL

Like most Chinese, my parents accepted death as part of the cycle of life and, in their practical way, prepared for it ahead of time. I remember them choosing their gravesite when I was only a child. Now our whole family gathers there every year around *Ching Ming*, Chinese Memorial Day, to celebrate my parents' lives, reflect on growing older, and observe how our children have grown and blossomed the past year.

Everyone comes, bearing food and flowers that we've picked from our gardens to blend into gaudy bouquets. The gravesite is laden with a whole barbecued pig, boxes of dim sum and sweets, a cooked chicken with head and feet, and a pair of pan-fried whole fish surrounded by fried tofu. Ceremonial bowls of rice, chopsticks, cups of tea, and shot glasses of whiskey are laid out as well.

We take turns bowing to each gravestone, then pour a sip of tea and whiskey into the ground for my parents. We present new husbands, wives, and babies, and murmur updates on events of the past year—all the things that would have made them happy. Nor are we above asking for things like a good crop, a raise, or luck in Reno. As a fitting conclusion, we pack up all the food and take it to the nearest relative's home for a feast.

More than Chinese New Year, Thanksgiving, or Christmas, *Ching Ming* unifies, comforts, and renews us. I look at everyone there and I am proud of the legacy my parents left.

Moon Festival

In September, all our relatives exchanged boxes of moon cakes to celebrate the festival of the harvest moon. A moon cake's texture is unlike any American cake or pastry. Wrapped in a thin layer of glazed pastry and formed in a special mold, the cakes are made of dense, sweetened lotus seed paste, black bean paste, or a mélange of shredded pork, coconut, candied fruit, and nuts. A preserved egg yolk, representing the harvest moon, is placed in the center, so that when the cake is cut (always quartered) each piece has its own pretty bit of yolk.

Although moon cakes were expensive, they were considered too difficult to make at home. Our parents always made a special trip to San Francisco to purchase them. The best part of those trips was that our parents would also buy us each one of the large, fat cookies in the shape of Buddha that were only available right before the Moon Festival. Multicolored candies were sprinkled on his glazed tummy and a loop of red string emerged from his head. If our parents were a little late making their trip, we might have to settle for smaller cookies in the shape of a fish, or a pig in its own bright plastic cage, or worse yet be deprived altogether for that year.

Some of us children ate our cookies quickly, unable to resist. Others looped the string around a wrist or shirt button and stretched out the pleasure for days, comparing to see who had more left. Surprisingly, our mothers did not seem to mind our getting the grease from the cookies on our shirts.

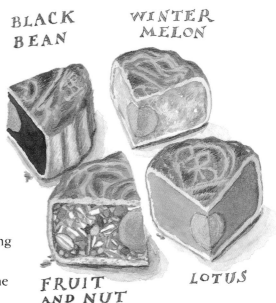

BLACK BEAN

WINTER MELON

FRUIT AND NUT

LOTUS

BUDDHA COOKIES were best. We got FISH if Buddhas had sold out, and PIGS in BASKETS if the fish were gone.

Buddha cookies

MAKES SIX 4-INCH COOKIES

These are not as elegant as the bakery version, since those require fancy molds, but they are otherwise close in texture and flavor, and children will still have fun with them. You can also form the dough into fish shapes.

¾	cup packed light brown sugar	¼	teaspoon baking soda
2	tablespoons water		Red cotton string
1	tablespoon vegetable oil	1	egg, lightly beaten, for glaze
1	large egg		About 1 teaspoon multicolored candy
2	cups all-purpose flour		sprinkles

In a large bowl, whisk together the brown sugar, water, oil, and egg.

Sift together the flour and baking soda. With a wooden spoon, stir about 1 cup of the flour mixture into the wet ingredients. Continue adding the flour about

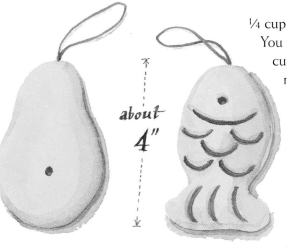

about 4"

BUDDHA **FISH**

¼ cup at a time until all is incorporated. You will have to knead in the last ¼ cup. The dough should be stiff but not dry.

Preheat the oven to 350°F. Oil a cookie sheet.

To shape the Buddhas, divide the dough into 6 portions. Roll one portion of the dough into a ball. Flatten it to about ½ inch thick and elongate it into a pear shape. Fold a 9-inch piece of red cotton string in half. With the blunt end of a bamboo skewer, insert the cut ends of the string about ¾ inch into the top of the narrower end of the cookie. Pinch the dough closed over the hole. Lay the cookie on the cookie sheet. With the blunt end of the bamboo skewer, poke a deep hole in the center of the round part of the pear to make the belly button.

To shape a fish, roll one portion of the dough into a ball. Flatten it out about ½ inch thick and form it into a fat fish shape. Fold a piece of string in half. With the blunt end of a bamboo skewer, insert the cut ends of the string about ¾ inch into the head end. Pinch the dough closed over the hole. Lay the cookie on the cookie sheet. You can make fish scales by indenting the dough with an inverted spoon. With the blunt end of a bamboo skewer, poke a deep hole to make an eye.

Using a pastry brush or your fingertips, brush the cookies with the beaten egg. Sprinkle a few candy sprinkles on each.

Bake on the middle rack of the oven for 20 to 25 minutes. Transfer the cookies to a wire rack and cool completely before storing in an airtight container.

SWEETS

Chinese sweets are most often offered for breakfast, as snacks, as a selection from a dim sum cart, or as an accompaniment to tea for afternoon guests.

Although dessert is not traditional after a Chinese dinner, the recipes in this chapter can be served with wedges of oranges and hot tea for a sweet finish.

In addition, look for the following sweet treats elsewhere in the book. *Lek doi* (page 68) are hollow balls of rice flour and sweet potato dough enclosing a hint of sweet or savory filling and deep-fried for a standard birthday or holiday treat. Baked Sweet *Bao* (page 64), yeast bread buns enclosing a bit of lotus seed paste or sweet bean paste, are a popular dim sum offering.

Almond cookies

MAKES ABOUT 36 COOKIES

These crisp cookies are not too sweet and make a welcome afternoon pick-me-up or simple dessert with tea. The original recipe called for lard, but we prefer vegetable shortening. These will keep several days in an airtight tin.

1	cup vegetable shortening (or lard)	1¾	cups all-purpose flour
1¼	cups sugar	1	teaspoon baking powder
1	large egg	¼	teaspoon baking soda
½	teaspoon vanilla extract	36	blanched almonds
1	teaspoon almond extract		

Preheat the oven to 375°F.

With an electric beater, cream together the shortening and sugar until fluffy. Crack the egg into a small bowl, beat it well with a fork, and reserve 1 tablespoonful. Beat the rest of the egg and the vanilla and almond extracts into the sugar mixture until well combined.

Sift together the flour, baking powder and baking soda onto a piece of wax paper. Add to the creamed mixture and stir until just blended. The dough will be crumbly but should hold together when squeezed into a ball.

Form the dough into 32 to 36 balls, each about 1 inch in diameter. Place them 2 inches apart on ungreased cookie sheets. Press a blanched almond into the center of each ball. The edges of the dough will crack slightly. With your fingertips or a small pastry brush, brush the tops of the cookies lightly with the reserved beaten egg.

Bake 12 to 15 minutes, until the cookies are golden brown. With a spatula, remove the cookies to a rack to cool. Store in an airtight container.

Sesame Cookies

Similar to Almond Cookies, opposite, these cookies are a crisp, sweet treat for the end of a meal.

½	*cup vegetable shortening*
½	*cup plus 1 tablespoon sugar*
1	*large egg*
½	*teaspoon vanilla extract*
1¼	*cups all-purpose flour*
½	*teaspoon baking powder*
⅛	*teaspoon baking soda*
	About ⅓ cup sesame seeds

Preheat the oven to 400° F.

With an electric beater, cream together the shortening and sugar until fluffy. Add the egg and beat well. Beat in the vanilla.

Sift together the flour, baking powder, and baking soda onto a piece of wax paper. Add to the creamed mixture and stir until just blended.

Form the dough into balls, using a scant teaspoon of dough for each one. Place about 2 tablespoons of the sesame seeds in a pie pan. Roll the balls, about 12 at a time, in the seeds, replenishing the pan with seeds as necessary. Place the balls 1½ inches apart on ungreased cookie sheets.

Bake for 10 to 12 minutes, until the cookies are light golden brown. With a spatula, remove the cookies to a rack to cool. Store in an airtight container.

Custard Tarts (Don Tot)

MAKES 12 INDIVIDUAL TARTS

These individual custard tarts have a crisp, thin shell that requires no rolling. Custard Tarts are often a sweet choice on a dim sum cart and they are always popular with children.

TART SHELLS
- 2 cups all-purpose flour
- Pinch of salt
- ½ cup vegetable oil
- ¼ cup milk

CUSTARD
- 1½ cups milk
- 3 eggs
- ⅓ cup sugar
- 1 teaspoon vanilla extract

You will need 12 individual fluted tart tins or brioche tins with a 2½-ounce capacity. You can also use standard muffin tins.

To make the tart shells, mix the flour and salt together with a fork in a large bowl. Add the oil and milk and stir gently with a fork until the dough is just blended. If the dough seems very dry, add a few more drops of milk. (Do not overstir or overwork the dough or the tart shells will become tough.)

Divide the dough into 12 equal pieces. Put one piece in each ungreased tart tin. With your fingertips, shape the dough into the tin so that it covers the inside evenly all the way to the top. (Shape the dough in the muffin tins evenly to within ¼ inch of the top.) Cover and refrigerate the tart shells while you make the custard. (Tart shells may be made 1 day ahead and refrigerated, or up to 1 week ahead and frozen, tightly wrapped.)

Preheat the oven to 400°F.

To make the filling, scald the milk and cool to lukewarm. Beat the eggs with a wire whisk. Mix in the sugar, cooled milk, and vanilla until well blended.

Space the prepared tart tins evenly on a cookie sheet. Ladle about ¼ cup of the custard mixture almost all the way to the top into each tart shell. (The custard will expand while cooking, then contract again as it cools.) Leftover custard may be baked in a small oiled ovenproof bowl along with the tarts.

Bake 25 to 30 minutes, or until the tart shells are browned and a knife inserted into the custard comes out clean.

Cool the tarts on a rack. Remove them from the tins when cooled. (Invert an individual tin briefly over one hand, remove the tin, and flip the tart right side up again immediately. Use a table knife to remove the tarts from a muffin tin.) Cover and refrigerate the tarts if you do not plan to serve them within 2 hours.

Hot Tea

When we were growing up, tea was always available at home. Kept hot in a porcelain teapot nestled in an insulated basket, it was ready at a moment's notice to restore our spirits, quench our thirst, and stimulate good conversation.

To make tea, measure ½ to 1 teaspoon of loose tea leaves per cup of water. Bring cold water to a boil, but do not let it boil more than a few seconds or the tea will taste flat. Scald the teapot with boiling water, then pour the water out. Put the tea leaves in the teapot, then immediately add the water. Cover and steep 3 to 5 minutes, or to the desired strength. To keep tea hot, you can store it in a traditional Chinese insulated basket or in a thermos that has been scalded as above. You may put the loose tea in a mesh tea ball before you put it into the teapot, then remove it once the tea has steeped to your liking. Otherwise, you may want to strain the leaves out of the tea with a tea strainer as you pour it into the thermos or cups.

TEA IS KEPT HOT IN A BASKET PADDED WITH CLOTH SCRAPS. A BRIGHT FABRIC IS CUT TO FIT THE TEAPOT SNUGLY. EVEN THE LID IS PADDED.

coconut walnut pastries (Yook Jun Soo)

When Ellen's mother baked these by trayfuls, we could hardly wait for them to cool to bite into the flaky pastry.

FILLING

- 2 tablespoons plus 1 teaspoon sugar
- ¼ cup plus 1 tablespoon water
- ⅓ cup finely chopped walnuts
- 2 cups sweetened shredded or flaked coconut (7 ounces)
- 1 tablespoon glutinous rice flour

FIRST DOUGH

- 1¾ cups all-purpose flour
- 3 tablespoons sugar
- 3 tablespoons vegetable shortening (or lard)
- ½ cup cold water

SECOND DOUGH

- 1 cup all-purpose flour
- 5 tablespoons vegetable shortening (or lard)
- 1 egg for glaze

Dissolve the sugar for the filling in ¼ cup of the water over medium heat in a nonstick wok or skillet. Stir in the walnuts, coconut, and rice flour and cook over medium heat for 1 minute, stirring constantly. Add the remaining 1 tablespoon water and cook 1 minute longer. Set the mixture aside to cool.

Sift together the flour and sugar for the first dough into a medium bowl. Cut in the shortening with a pastry cutter or 2 forks until it is evenly distributed. Mix in the cold water with a fork, then knead the dough lightly 10 to 12 times to form a ball. Let the dough rest in the bowl, covered with a damp towel, while you make the second dough.

For the second dough, combine the flour and shortening with a pastry cutter or 2 forks. Knead the mixture lightly in the bowl to form a soft dough. Scoop out a heaping teaspoon at a time and squeeze the dough into 24 balls. Set aside.

Preheat the oven to 375°F.

Pat the first dough into a circle and flatten it slightly. Cut it into 8 pie-shaped wedges. Form each wedge into a cylinder and cut into thirds. You should end up

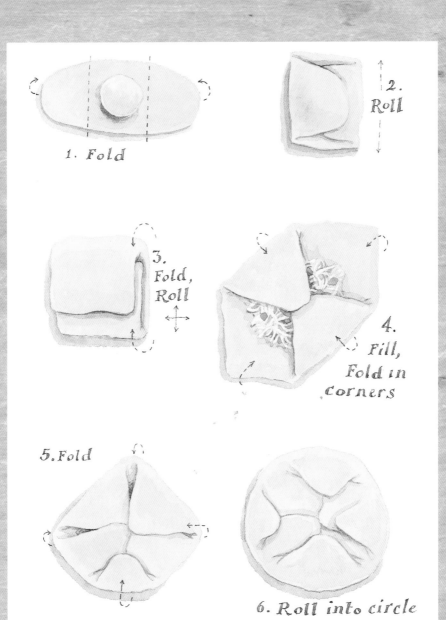

1. Fold

2. Roll

3. Fold, Roll

4. Fill, Fold in corners

5. Fold

6. Roll into circle

with 24 portions in all. Keep the dough covered with a damp cloth.

Take one portion of the first dough and lightly shape it into a ball. On a lightly floured board, roll it out in one direction to form an oval about 4 inches long and 1 ½ to 2 inches wide.

Center a ball of the second dough over this and overlap the long ends of the oval over the ball to enclose it. Roll the dough crosswise until it is about 4 inches long. Fold the long sides toward the middle, overlapping the ends slightly. Roll the dough into a rounded 4-inch square.

Scoop a heaping tablespoon of filling into the center. Bring in the opposite corners of the dough and pinch them together. Fold in the open corners to enclose the filling completely. (You do not have to pinch the dough tightly. The next step will close the dough over the filling.) With the pinched side up, roll the pastry out gently to flatten the seams and form a circle about 3 inches in diameter. Place the pastries, seam side down, 1 inch apart on an ungreased cookie sheet. (The coconut or walnuts may be pressed almost through the dough when you roll it. Because it is a dry filling, you do not have to be concerned about it leaking out.)

Beat the egg with a fork in a small bowl. With a pastry brush or your fingertips, brush some egg on the top of each pastry.

Bake 15 to 20 minutes, until the pastries are golden. Cool the pastries on a rack. Store in an airtight container. Cut the pastries into halves or quarters to serve.

Steamed Sponge Cake

MAKES ONE 8-INCH ROUND CAKE

This simple, light cake is best served hot or warm. It goes well with tea after a Chinese meal and makes a good sweet choice on a dim sum tray.

2 large eggs, at room temperature	Dash of salt
⅓ cup firmly packed light brown sugar	Dash of cinnamon (optional)
½ teaspoon vanilla extract	⅔ cup all-purpose flour
½ teaspoon almond extract	¼ teaspoon baking powder

Oil and flour an 8-inch round cake pan. Set a rack in a pot and add water to a depth of 1½ to 2 inches. (If you are using a steamer, fill the lower tier half full with water.)

With an electric mixer, beat the eggs at high speed for 1 minute. Add the brown sugar and beat until very thick, 4 to 5 minutes. Beat in the vanilla and almond extracts, salt, and cinnamon, if using.

Start heating the water over high heat.

Sift together the flour and baking powder and fold them lightly into the egg mixture with a spatula.

Pour the batter into the pan, smoothing it evenly to the edges with a spatula. When the water in the pot is boiling, set the pan on the rack (or on the upper tier of the steamer) and steam for 10 minutes over high heat. The cake is done when it springs back to the touch or when a toothpick inserted in the middle comes out clean.

Let the cake cool 5 minutes in the pan on a rack. Cut the cake into diamond shapes and serve hot or warm.

A groom's family has many obligations before a wedding. One of them is delivering an assortment of small, rich cakes called *beng* to the bride's family for an engagement feast. Most of the cakes offered by a prospective groom to the family of the bride-to-be are similar to pastries, with a thin dough enclosing a rich filling of candied fruit, nuts, coconut, candied melon, or sweet lotus seed paste. The exception is a light sponge cake baked in special molds.

The greater the quantity of cakes delivered—and the more guests anticipated for the wedding—the better the groom's family looks, and the more the bride's family is expected to provide in the way of a dowry of clothing, gold jewelry, and sometimes even land or a house.

Different regions dictate the kinds of *beng* that are to be delivered. Some, identical to the cakes made for the Moon Festival, are considered too difficult to make at home, especially in the enormous quantities that are usually required. For example, my father delivered three thousand *beng* to my mother's family.

In America, this tradition has evolved to include the presentation of a whole roast pig to the bride's family as part of the *beng* feast, but in China a pig was not delivered until after the wedding, and then only when a bride's virginity was proven. The public humiliation that resulted from the significant absence of a roast pig was a Chinese-style deterrent to premarital passion.

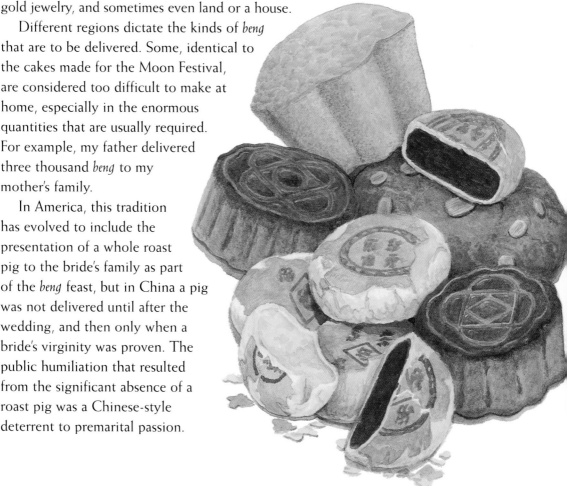

Engagement Cakes

MAKES 6 CAKES

These moist sponge cakes are baked in molds that always looked like big blossoms to us. The rich, eggy cake is light and not too sweet; it is especially nice topped with sweetened fresh or frozen strawberries, though that is not traditional. If you can't find the special molds in an Asian kitchenware store, the cakes may be baked in paper-lined muffin tins for 25 to 30 minutes or 9-inch round cake pans for 30 to 35 minutes. They are best when served on the same day they are made.

2 cups cake flour	¼ teaspoon cream of tartar
1 cup sugar	½ cup vegetable oil
1 tablespoon baking powder	¾ cup water
6 large eggs, at room temperature	1 teaspoon almond extract

Preheat the oven to 350°F. Oil and flour 6 1¾-cup cake molds and shake out any excess flour.

Sift together the flour, ½ cup of the sugar, and the baking powder into a bowl.

Separate the egg whites from the yolks into 2 large bowls. Add the cream of tartar to the whites and beat with an electric mixer at medium speed until they are frothy. Add the remaining ½ cup of sugar and beat at high speed until the whites are stiff but not dry. Set aside. In the other bowl, combine the oil, water, and almond extract with the egg yolks. Beat about 30 seconds to blend.

Lightly stir the flour mixture into the yolk mixture until smooth. Fold in the beaten egg whites. Spoon the batter into the prepared molds and arrange the molds on a cookie sheet with space between each. Bake until the tops are lightly browned and spring back when lightly touched, about 35 to 40 minutes.

Allow the cakes to cool in the molds on a rack 5 to 10 minutes, then use a table knife to carefully release the cakes from the molds. Turn out onto a rack and let the cakes cool completely.

Just One More Meal

ANNABEL

One golden fall afternoon as I took a walk, delicious aromas wafted from a nearby Chinese restaurant. For a brief magical moment, time stood still. The comforting smell of familiar food and the nip in the air took me back to when I was a young girl in Sacramento, coming home from school. I saw the past very clearly and the images were so powerful, I stopped in my tracks.

I remembered how I used to daydream all the way home from school and how, as I approached our house, the fragrance of the wonderful dishes my parents were cooking would make me feel safe and happy. I remembered how that aroma pulled me from my reveries and how I bounded up the steps, eagerly looking forward to dinner. I saw our family gathered in the dining room, Father sitting proudly at the head of the table and Mother fussing over my sister and me, giving us the best pieces of meat.

How I miss them! What I would give now for just one more meal with my parents. How I long to go back in time to savor those moments I didn't fully appreciate as a child, to look into my parents' kind faces one more time, to hear their voices and to taste their food once again.

MENUS

Careful planning is an important part of creating a Chinese meal. One should consider how many dishes to serve, how to balance flavors, textures, and colors, and how to coordinate cooking techniques and timing. Here are some suggestions to help you with your planning.

Many of the serving yields for our recipes specify "as part of a Chinese meal," which assumes three or four dishes for four to six people or four to five dishes for six to eight people. However, a dish that serves four to six in a multicourse meal will usually serve two to three as a main course with steamed rice. A dish that serves six to eight will usually serve three to four as a main course with steamed rice. Noodle-based dishes are generally served alone, usually for lunch rather than dinner, and are not usually combined with a rice-based meal.

In planning a menu, balance your choices of vegetables, fish, seafood, poultry, and meats to offer your guests an interesting variety of flavors, colors, and textures.

Think about utilizing your burner and oven space most efficiently. To shorten overall preparation time, read through the recipes carefully in advance to see what steps and techniques are involved. Consider how many dishes will require last-minute stir-frying, chopping, or sauce thickening. To eliminate too much last-minute cooking, select a variety of stir-fry dishes, steamed dishes, and oven-cooked dishes and dishes you can make ahead of time. Although older relatives smile at this, we often end up tacking a cooking schedule to the refrigerator door when undertaking a multicourse meal.

Finally, when the food is on the table, relax and enjoy yourself and your guests.

SEVERAL TWO-DISH HOMESTYLE DINNERS FOR 3 TO 4 PEOPLE (SERVE WITH STEAMED RICE)

Steamed Fish in Black Bean Sauce
Asparagus with Soy Dressing

◆

Black Bean Spareribs
Chinese Broccoli Tossed with Oyster Sauce and Oils

◆

Steamed Minced Pork with Black Beans
Eggs Foo Yung with Chinese Chives

◆

Pan-Fried Prawns in Ketchup Sauce
Sesame Spinach

◆

Steamed Chicken with Cloud Ears and Black Mushrooms
Chinese Broccoli Tossed with Oyster Sauce and Oils

TWO HOMESTYLE DINNERS FOR 6 TO 8 PEOPLE (SERVE WITH STEAMED RICE)

Black Bean Spareribs
Roast Chicken
Steamed Eggs with Clams
Asparagus with Soy Dressing

◆

Watercress Soup
Stand Back Chicken
Pan-Fried Prawns in the Shell
Oyster Beef with Broccoli

DISHES THAT MAY BE MADE OR STARTED AHEAD FOR A BUSY WEEKNIGHT

Wonton Soup (freeze ahead)
Jook (all varieties except fish)
Black Mushrooms in Oyster Sauce
Stewed Short Ribs, Oxtail Stew, or Beef Stew
Beef Tongue
Low Hop Joe's Soy Sauce Chicken with Variations
(make the sauce ahead for simple last-minute cooking)

Simple Lunch with a Friend

Wonton Soup or Chinese Chicken Salad or Noodles in Broth
Hot tea with Almond Cookies or Sesame Cookies and seasonal fruit

Elaborate Birthday Lunch
(Like the Ones We Used to Have)

Batter-Fried Chicken
Uncle Bill's Chow Mein
Siu Mai
Baked *Char Siu Bao* and Baked Sweet *Bao*
Barbecued Flank Steak on Skewers
Lek Doi

Two Elaborate Dinners for Someone Special
and a Table Full of Good Compnay
(Serve with Plenty of Steamed Rice and Hot Tea
and Finish with a Plate of Sliced Sweet Oranges)

Green Loofah Squash with Prawns
Lobster Tails in Special Sauce
Oyster Beef with Broccoli
Chicken in Foil or Parchment
Boned Stuffed Duck

◆

Winter Melon Soup
Simple Steamed Fish with Garlic
Sweet-and-Sour Pork
Black Mushrooms in Oyster Sauce
Low Hop Joe's Soy Sauce Chicken
Asparagus Tossed with Soy Sauce and Oil

Kids' Dinner Favorites

Fried Rice
Chicken in Foil or Parchment (either variation)
Chow Mein (all varieties)
Stir-Fried Rice Noodles
Batter-Fried Chicken or Batter-Fried Prawns

Curve fits curve of a wok

SCOOP

Chinese Wire Mesh Strainer

SIEVE

CLEAVERS
Different weights for different tasks

LONG CHOPSTICKS for cooking

MESH TEA BALL

TEA STRAINER

LID

ENAMEL PAN for vinegar and other acidic food

WOK

WOK RING

condiment dish

TEA CUP

NAPKIN

RICE BOWL

PLATE

CHOPSTICKS

Porcelain spoon

PLACE SETTING

EQUIPMENT

CHOPSTICKS Besides standard chopsticks used for eating, special long chopsticks handy for deep-frying or stir-frying are available at Asian kitchenware stores.

CLEAVERS come in various weights for different tasks. Thin blades are for cutting vegetables. Heavier blades can chop through bones. Unless a cleaver is stainless steel, it should be washed and dried immediately after using to avoid rust.

Besides performing like any other knife, the end of the cleaver handle may be used like a pestle, and the flat blade is used to scoop up and transport chopped food. The flat side of the blade may also be used to smash a peeled clove of garlic on a cutting board.

CONDIMENT DISHES are usually 3 to 4 inches in diameter, and are used to hold small amounts of soy sauce, chili oil, seasoned salt, mustard, or other mixtures for dipping. Set enough condiment dishes around a table so that there is one within reach of each diner.

ENAMEL PAN Heavy iron cookware with a durable enamel coating is the best choice when a recipe contains vinegar or acidic ingredients that could react with aluminum or other metals and give the food an off-flavor. Also good for long, slow-cooked, and braised dishes.

HEATPROOF DISHES for steaming include tempered glass, stainless steel round pans or pie pans, or porcelain baking dishes. Choose dishes about 8 to 9 inches in diameter that will fit comfortably into the steamer and 1¼ inches deep to catch juices during cooking. Remove dishes from the steamer carefully, using a plate lifter (see below) and insulated oven mitts.

PLACE SETTING Traditional Chinese place setting consists of a dessert-sized plate, rice bowl, porcelain spoon (if soup is served), teacup, napkin, and a pair of chopsticks.

PLATE LIFTER For removing a heatproof dish from a pot or steamer, this inexpensive device, available at many Asian markets or kitchenware stores, is invaluable. Be sure also to support the dish from below with an insulated oven mitt as soon as you have lifted the plate out of the pot or steamer, and only use the plate lifter to pick up the dish so that you can hold it more securely with oven mitts or pot holders.

PLATTERS Have a variety on hand, both large and small sizes. When serving many guests, divide a finished dish among two or more smaller platters or plates. Besides avoiding the inconvenience of passing large, heavy platters all through dinner, this allows guests to choose from the whole variety of dishes as desired.

SCOOP A long-handled, shallow, ladlelike tool. Holding a scoop in one hand and a spatula in the other hand helps remove ingredients from a wok more easily.

SPATULA This special long-handled metal spatula has a curved blade to fit the curve of a wok and is excellent for stir-frying. Do not use it in a nonstick wok or other nonstick pans, as it will damage the finish.

STEAMERS It is easy to create an improvised steamer from the pots you have on hand already. Use a pot large enough to hold a heatproof dish on a rack, with enough room all around for you to remove the dish with insulated oven mitts or a plate lifter. Set the rack in the pot and add water to a depth of 1½ to 2 inches. Racks are available at Asian kitchenware stores, or you can devise one from a 6-ounce tuna can with both ends removed. Bring the water to a boil, then set the heatproof dish on the rack. Generally, food is steamed at high heat and the pot must be replenished with boiling water after about 20 minutes so that it does not boil dry. A large metal funnel is useful for pouring additional water into the pot without splashing it into the dish. (Hold the funnel with an oven mitt, as it will get quite hot.)

Asian kitchenware stores and some Asian markets also sell tiered steamers. The lower tier is for water; the upper tier or tiers have perforated bottoms and are used for the food. The tiers fit together tightly and are topped by a lid with a vent. The advantage of a steamer is that it may be filled with more water than most pots, so for long steaming times, you will not have to replenish the pot with boiling water as often.

An alternative to a pot or metal steamer, if you are lucky enough to find or inherit one, is a bamboo steamer. These fit snugly inside the circumference of a wok. The wok is filled with water to just below the steamer's bottom edge. The water is then brought to a boil before the steamer is set in place.

Bamboo imparts a wonderful scent to the kitchen and food as it steams. The ingenious steamers, made without a bit of metal or other material, are surprisingly efficient at trapping in steam. The ones we use have been in intermittent service for over thirty-five years.

STEAMING RACKS

PLATE LIFTERS

GRIP FIRMLY

WOK INSETS for steaming

TUNA CAN open at both ends

HEATPROOF DISHES

DEEP DISH

GLASS PIE PLATE

CAKE PAN

heatproof dish

} 1½" to 2" water

rack

TIERED STEAMER

BAMBOO STEAMER

WOK

STRAINERS A wire mesh strainer, available at many Asian kitchenware stores or Asian markets, has a heatproof bamboo handle. Different-sized bowls are used for different tasks; choose one that fits comfortably in your wok and is large enough to easily hold what you are cooking. Mesh sieves are handy for scooping up stray bits from deep-frying oil. Slotted spoons may be used for smaller items or in combination with a large strainer to help hold large pieces of food.

WOK The versatile wok is used to stir-fry, deep-fry, braise, and steam. For all-purpose cooking, a 14-inch wok works well. Stainless steel and nonstick woks do not need to be seasoned. However, a carbon steel wok must be seasoned before it is used the first time. Wash it thoroughly in hot water and detergent and scrub off any protective oil the manufacturer may have applied. Dry the wok and put it over low heat. Put a tablespoon or two of oil into the wok and immediately wipe it all over the inside surface. The paper towel will have a black residue on it. Repeat the process several times with a clean paper towel until the towel no longer shows residue after wiping; remove from the heat. Your wok is now seasoned and ready to use. Once seasoned, it should not be washed with abrasive cleaners or cleaned with metal scrubbers or steel wool. Some cooks believe that a seasoned wok should never be washed in detergent, but we use detergent, rinse thoroughly, and dry the wok immediately over high heat for a few seconds to prevent rust.

Woks should have snugly fitting lids that rest just inside the rim. Most are somewhat domed to accommodate a steamed dish on a rack.

WOK STAND OR WOK RING A round-bottomed wok needs a special stand to stabilize the wok over a burner. Be sure to buy it when you buy your wok. Flat-bottomed woks do not need a stand.

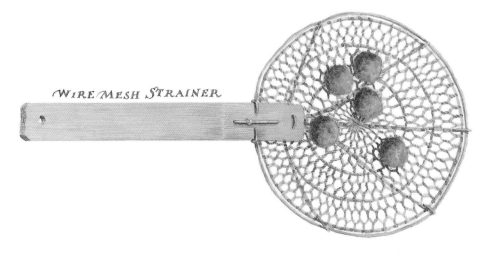

WIRE MESH STRAINER

TECHNIQUES

When we were about to leave home for college, we tried to get information from our mothers about specific quantities of ingredients for our favorite recipes. More often than not, we were told, "Use your eye."

By that, of course, our mothers meant that we needed to develop an instinct, to be able to sense the correct amounts of seasonings just by looking at the amount of meat or vegetables we planned to use. We wanted to hear half-teaspoons, ounces, or quarter-cups.

When we tried to get measurements from Uncle Bill for his chow mein, he gave instructions like, "Half a Chinese rice bowl," or "Drizzle oyster sauce two times around the wok," or when we pressed for a cooking time, "Until it looks right!"

The adults had traded many of these same recipes back and forth among themselves, but their instinctive tendencies to season to their own tastes made their dishes taste distinctly different. We got to recognize their individual styles.

Consequently, proportions listed in our recipes should be regarded as a starting point. The exceptions to this imprecision of measuring are breads and cakes, where the best results come from careful measuring.

BLANCHING preserves the color and crispness of vegetables and reduces their cooking time if they are to be added to a stir-fry dish later. This step may be done ahead so that finishing a dish will take less time and effort later. To blanch vegetables, bring a pot of water to a boil, then add whole or cut vegetables and cook just a few minutes; the time will vary by vegetable, but they should *not* be soft and tender. Drain the vegetables in a colander. Unless you are using them immediately, rinse them under cold water to stop the cooking and keep the color bright.

BRAISING A long, slow method for cooking foods in liquid that creates very flavorful, tender results. Brown fish, poultry, or meat over high heat first to seal in the juices, then add the seasonings and liquid, cover tightly, and cook over very low heat until the ingredients are tender.

DEEP-FRYING For the best results, fried food should be cooked in oil main-
tained at a consistent and appropriate level. Too low a temperature will cause
food to become oil laden and soggy; too high a temperature may cause the food
to brown too quickly before it is cooked through. We recommend using a candy
and deep-frying thermometer, clipped to the side of a wok so that it reaches
about halfway into the oil.

   Be very careful around hot oil, since it will reach temperatures around 370° F.
Your wok or pan must have a steady base so that it will not tip and spill flamma-
ble oil. Some cooks invert the wok ring over the burner to make a wider, steadier
base for the wok. Do not overfill a wok or pan; the oil should reach no higher
than 2½ to 3 inches from the rim. When in doubt, use a larger pan. Wear an
apron, keep your hair and sleeves or other clothing as far away from the oil as
possible, and use long-handled utensils. Lower food quickly but gently into the
oil. Keep children away from the stove while you are working and while the oil is
cooling afterward, and don't leave the wok unattended while you are deep-frying.
Use a thermometer and lower the heat if the oil temperature exceeds 370° F. It is a
good idea to keep a fire extinguisher in your kitchen for emergencies.

MARINATING Many Chinese dishes use marinades to give quickly cooked fish,
poultry, or meat more flavor when cooked. Observe the recommended marinating
times closely because overmarinating may cause the fish, poultry, or meat to
become overly tenderized or salty and the texture of the dish may change.

SIMMERING When we specify simmering, we mean cooking at the lowest temperature possible on the stovetop. Slow cooking serves to blend flavors and ten-
derize poultry and meat.

SOAKING is required to rehydrate many dried ingredients used in Chinese
cooking. We list soaking instructions at the beginning of our recipes so that the
ingredients will be ready as you proceed.

STEAMING See STEAMERS (page 190).

STIR-FRYING Similar to sautéing, stir-frying involves tossing marinated, quick-
cooking, or partially precooked ingredients together over very high heat. It is
important to cut your ingredients into similar-sized pieces and add them to the
wok in the order listed in the recipes so that they will all be cooked through
when the dish is finished. Always heat the wok first, then heat the oil; this step
minimizes sticking. Scoop under the food with a spatula and turn it over constantly. Add sauce or liquids only after the food is partially cooked or it will boil
rather than fry. To thicken the sauce, push the ingredients to one side and stir in a
cornstarch and water mixture as specified to the bubbling hot liquid.

GLOSSARY

Those entries marked with an asterisk (*) are sold primarily at Asian markets; all other ingredients can be found in the Asian section of a well-stocked supermarket and in many gourmet stores.

**ARROW~
HEAD**

ANISE SEEDS Similar to fennel seeds, these narrow, wheat-colored seeds have a licorice flavor. Not to be confused with star anise.

*ARROWHEADS Starchy corms. Usually available in winter. (See illustration, page 163.)

*BAMBOO LEAVES, DRIED Sold in 14- to 16-ounce packages containing over 200 leaves. Soaked and boiled, they become pliable wrappers that impart a subtle flavor to the foods they enclose.

BAMBOO SHOOTS Tender new growth from a variety of bamboo. Used in stir-fried dishes, stuffings, and soup. Sold in cans, sliced, shredded, or whole.

**BAMBOO
SHOOTS**

*BARBECUED PIGS' FEET Taken from a whole Chinese roast pig, these are available at some Chinese take-out delicatessens. Do not substitute ham hocks.

*BEAN CURD, FERMENTED Made from soybeans fermented in wine, salt, and sometimes chilies. Sold in jars sometimes labeled Wet Bean Curd. Its salty, pungent flavor is used as a seasoning or marinade ingredient, or as a condiment for rice. Ivory-colored and saltier than red bean curd.

*BEAN CURD, RED Made from soybeans fermented in a reddish brine made of wine, red rice, and salt and sold in jars sometimes labeled Wet Bean Curd. More mellow than fermented bean curd, its salty, pungent flavor is used as a seasoning ingredient or as a condiment for rice. An excellent flavoring for stews.

*BEAN CURD STICKS (or dried bean flour skins) Brittle sticks about 10 inches long. After soaking and cooking, they become chewy. Used in stews, jook, and vegetarian dishes.

BEAN THREADS (or cellophane noodles or vermicelli) Clear and wiry, they are sold dried and require soaking before cooking. Do not confuse with wheat-based vermicelli.

BEAN CURD STICK

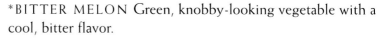

BEAN THREADS

*BITTER MELON Green, knobby-looking vegetable with a cool, bitter flavor.

BLACK MUSHROOMS (or shiitake mushrooms) Though available fresh and dried, the dried are more readily available and have a more intense flavor. The most expensive grade, with a deeply ridged starlike pattern on their caps, has the most pleasant texture. Less expensive grades are usually used chopped or combined into fillings.

*BROWN BEAN SAUCE (or yellow bean sauce) A richly flavored, salty sauce used as a marinade ingredient and to season fish.

*BROWN SUGAR BARS (also called Brown Candy) Sold in 1-pound packages, the brittle brown bars may be chopped for fillings or melted for recipes. Brown sugar may be substituted when specified.

CARDAMOM An aromatic spice that is generally used in the whole pod rather than ground in Chinese cooking.

*CASSIA The bark of a tropical Asian tree; similar to cinnamon.

*CHAR SIU Marinated roasted pork, which you can make (pages 136–137) or buy at many Chinese take-out delicatessens. It is served sliced, as a course by itself, or stir-fried with vegetables or noodles, as a topping, or as a filling for Baked *Char Siu Bao* (page 62).

CHESTNUTS, DRIED These have a slightly sweet, smoky flavor and a delicate texture. Used in stuffings, stews, and *jeng*. They are already blanched, but must be soaked before cooking.

*CHINESE BLACK OLIVES Available in several varieties. Those we used for this book are seedless, very salty, and shaped like triangles. Do not substitute canned black olives or the sweet licorice-flavored, football-shaped Chinese black olives.

*CHINESE BROCCOLI (See *GAI LAN*.)

CHINESE FIVE-SPICE POWDER
Finely ground mixture of star anise, cassia or cinnamon, Sichuan peppercorns, cloves, and fennel.

*CHINESE SAUSAGES
Uncooked sausages with a rich, sweet flavor. Some varieties contain liver. There is no substitute for their unique flavor.

CHOW MEIN NOODLES
Medium-thin wheat noodles sold fresh or dried. Wheat-based vermicelli can sometimes be substituted, but do not substitute packaged fried chow mein noodles.

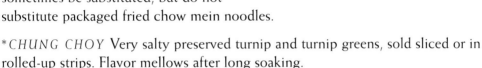

FENNEL STAR ANISE CLOVES CINNAMON SICHUAN PEPPERCORNS

chinese Five-Spice Powder
INGREDIENTS

*CHUNG CHOY Very salty preserved turnip and turnip greens, sold sliced or in rolled-up strips. Flavor mellows after long soaking.

CILANTRO (sometimes called Chinese parsley) A strongly flavored accent or garnish, this leafy green herb looks similar to flat-leaved Italian parsley, but its flavor is completely different. No substitute.

CLOUD EARS

*CLOUD EARS Dried black fungus with a crunchy texture and somewhat smoky flavor, more delicate than wood ears. Require soaking.

CORNSTARCH A fine, purified flour made from starchy corn used to dredge fish or meat before frying, or to help seal in juices when it is combined in a meat marinade, to bind ground meat, or to thicken sauces.

*CURING SALT (also called saltpeter) Sodium nitrate crystals used in cooking to give pork a pink color and hamlike texture.

DAIKON RADISHES Mild radishes that look like large, fat, white carrots. Served pickled or in stews. Also known as icicle radishes.

*DAIKON RADISHES, PRESERVED Packages are sometimes mislabeled "Preserved Turnip," but should be wrinkled, tan-colored strips about the thickness of a pencil, with no salt crystals. Sweet-and-salty flavor. Used in Savory Chinese Sausage Filling (page 70) or steamed with pork.

DOA POK Gluten is made from the protein in flour when the starch has been washed out, and is available in 1½-inch balls, already deep fried. It is used in vegetarian dishes such as Vegetarian Monks' Dish (page 162) because of its high protein content.

EGGS, SALTED PRESERVED Brine-cured eggs. The whites are very salty, but the yolks are bright gold with a rich, delicate flavor. Duck eggs are used for commercial salted preserved eggs, but you may preserve chicken eggs (page 47). Served hard-cooked and quartered as a condiment with rice or jook. Yolks are also used alone for savory and sweet dishes.

E-MEIN (or Yi mein or E-fu mein) Puffy cakes of pre-fried dried noodles; the pre-frying helps them hold their shape in broth. Do not substitute packaged deep-fried chow mein noodles.

FAT CHOY A black hairlike seaweed. Must be soaked and parboiled with ginger before use.

FISH, SALTED Very salty and pungent, used sparingly as a seasoning or condiment for minced pork, fried rice, or steamed rice. A brief soaking is required before cooking.

GAI LAN (Chinese broccoli) Has narrow stems, small flower heads, and a pleasant, slightly bitter flavor. (See illustration, page 75.)

GAN JUI (See POTASSIUM CARBONATE SOLUTION.)

GINGER A pungent, fibrous rhizome often used to counteract fishiness or balance other strong flavors with its own hot, spicy flavor. Do not substitute powdered ginger for the fresh root.

GINKGO NUTS The nut of the ginkgo tree. Must be shelled, then parboiled and skinned. Also available canned.

GLUTINOUS RICE (See RICE, GLUTINOUS.)

GLUTINOUS RICE FLOUR (See RICE FLOUR, GLUTINOUS.)

GINGER

HOISIN SAUCE A sweet and tangy sauce used in marinades and as a condiment. Sold in jars or cans. Once opened, transfer canned hoisin sauce to a glass jar for storage.

HOT CHILI OIL Vegetable oil infused with dried hot chilies. Used sparingly as a condiment. Sometimes also contains garlic.

*JUJUBES (or Chinese red dates) Grown on small shrubs, the fruit is always sold dried. They add a subtle sweet flavor to soups, stews, or celebration tea, or can be mashed for a sweet filling.

*LICORICE ROOT The sweet-flavored root of the licorice plant, sold dried and cut in diagonal slices. Used for Low Hop Joe's Soy Sauce Chicken (page 129).

LONG BEANS Thin, stringless green beans, about 16 to 24 inches long. Have a denser texture than other green beans and are usually stir-fried.

*LOOFAH SQUASH (or silk squash) A soft squash shaped like a long crookneck squash, but larger, with hard, prominent ribs and a dark green skin that must be peeled. Its flavor is similar to cucumber but it has a softer texture. Stir-fry or add to soups. (See illustration, page 82.)

*LOTUS ROOT A subaquatic sausage-shaped rhizome that is sold fresh. Usually used in stews. Sliced candied lotus root is used for New Year's snacks or to sweeten celebration tea.

*LOTUS SEEDS The seeds from the pods of a lotus flower. The dried seeds are sold blanched, but must be soaked and parboiled so the bitter green buds inside can be removed. Used in stir-fried dishes, soups, or stuffings, or can be mashed for a sweet filling.

LYCHEES (or lichees or litchis) Small round fruit with a bumpy reddish-brown hull, sweet, juicy white flesh, and smooth, glossy pit. Usually sold canned, but can be purchased fresh during midsummer. Used for sweet-and-sour dishes. Dried lychees are brown and chewy, and are eaten as a snack or sometimes added to soups.

NAPA (or nappa) CABBAGE Pale oval green cabbage that resembles romaine lettuce. Its crinkly leaves have a light texture and flavor.

OYSTER SAUCE Richly flavored thick brown sauce made from oyster juice, wheat, glutinous rice, salt, and sugar. Less salty than soy sauce.

*OYSTERS, DRIED Used sparingly to add texture and assertive flavor to soups, stews, or stir-fried or steamed dishes. Require soaking and cleaning before cooking.

*PEPPERCORNS, SICHUAN (also spelled Szechuan) Reddish-brown fragrant pods used in seasoned salt and five-spice powder.

*PICKLES, MIXED CHINESE Sold in jars, these sweet pickles may include shallots, and chunks of ginger, cucumber, carrots, and green papaya. They are used to add color and crunch to sweet-and-sour dishes or can be served alone as a refreshing side dish.

*PLUM SAUCE A mildly spicy, piquant sauce made from plum pulp, sugar, vinegar, chilies, ginger, and garlic. It is served as a condiment, often with duck, or as a marinade ingredient.

*POTASSIUM CARBONATE SOLUTION Used sparingly to give Sweet *Jeng* (page 44) its yellow color and distinctive flavor.

PRAWNS Larger than shrimp and preferred when they are to be served whole.

*RED BEAN CURD (See BEAN CURED, RED.)

RICE, GLUTINOUS (or sweet rice) Short-grained Japanese rice that has a sticky texture when cooked. No substitute—pearl rice and Calrose rice lack sufficient gluten.

RICE FLOUR, GLUTINOUS Made from glutinous sweet rice. Do not substitute rice flour from the health food store.

*RICE WINE Inexpensive wine used for cooking, with 12 to 18 percent alcohol content. Dry sherry may be substituted.

*ROCK SUGAR Large crystals of sugar, resembling quartz. White or brown sugar may be substituted when specified.

*SALTED FISH Pungent, salt-cured fish with a flavor similar to anchovies are available in many varieties. Generally, the higher the price, the better the flavor and texture.

*SAM CHING (or *San Cheng Chiew*) A distilled Chinese spirit, about 70 to 80 proof, that gives Whiskey Chicken (page 166) its potent reputation. For other recipes, use dry sherry or rice wine, with 12 to 18 percent alcohol content.

*SCALLOPS, DRIED Add a sweet, nutty flavor and chewy texture to soups, minced pork, or stir-fried dishes. Soaking required before cooking.

SESAME OIL (or toasted sesame oil) Extracted from cooked sesame seeds. Highly fragrant. Use sparingly for flavoring, not for frying. Chinese and Japanese brands

DRIED SCALLOPS

are interchangeable, but do not substitute cold-pressed sesame oil from the health food store.

SESAME SEEDS Used as a coating or garnish for savory or sweet dishes. Toasting enhances their flavor. Sometimes available in bulk at health food stores.

*SHALLOTS, PICKLED Sold in jars. Adds sweet flavor, a little bite, and crunchy texture to sweet-and-sour dishes.

*SHRIMP, DRIED Adds a salty concentrated shrimp flavor when used sparingly with meat, vegetables, soups, and rice. Soaking required before cooking.

SHRIMP, FRESH Less expensive than larger prawns. Used when ground or chopped and size is not important. Do not substitute cooked baby shrimp unless specified.

*SHRIMP PASTE (See SHRIMP SAUCE.)

*SHRIMP SAUCE (or shrimp paste) Adds a salty, pungent flavor similar to anchovies when used as a seasoning, usually for pork, shrimp, and eggplant dishes.

SICHUAN PEPPERCORNS (See PEPPERCORNS, SICHUAN.)

*SILK SQUASH (See LOOFAH SQUASH.)

*SIU MAI WRAPPERS (also known as sue gow wrappers or dumpling skins) Round, wheat-based wrappers that come approximately 70 to the one-pound package. Thinner than pot sticker wrappers and not interchangeable with them.

*SOO MOOK Thick splinters of this wood are used in Sweet Jeng (page 44) to give it a beet-red center and distinctive flavor. It is orange-colored when dry, cut in 3-inch lengths, and available in small packages.

SOY SAUCE A liquid flavoring made from fermented soybeans that is available in several grades or strengths. Light soy sauce is saltiest, used for dipping and cooking, except for stews where long cooking would concentrate its flavor too much. Dark soy sauce is thicker and moderately salty, usually used for stewing. Black soy sauce contains molasses. It is the heaviest and the least salty, and is used to add color rather than flavor. Japanese soy sauce is moderately salty and generally sweeter than Chinese brands.

STAR ANISE

STAR ANISE Eight-pointed star-shaped seed pods with licorice flavor.

SWEET RICE (See RICE, GLUTINOUS.)

*TANGERINE PEEL, DRIED Adds a citrus oil flavor to soups, stews, or stuffing. To make your own, cut a tangerine peel into quarters and let the pieces dry on a plate for about a week in a warm, dry place, until the peel becomes dark and leathery. When completely dry, the peels may be stored in an airtight container. Dried peel sometimes requires soaking.

TARO ROOT A tuber that is available in two different varieties. The flesh varies from creamy white to lavender with purple streaks. The larger variety is better for stews; small ones are more delicate in texture. Wear rubber gloves when peeling taro root because it contains calcium oxalate, which may cause your hands to itch. It should not be eaten raw. (See illustration, page 38.)

*TIGER LILY BUDS, DRIED (or lily flowers, dried lily buds, or golden needles) The dried whole lily flowers add a slightly smoky flavor and almost chewy texture to pork, poultry, soups, and vegetarian dishes. After soaking, remove the hard end.

TIGER LILY BUDS

TOFU, FRESH Made from finely ground soybeans squeezed into soft blocks. The recipes in this book use the firm variety, though the soft variety can be substituted when maintaining the shape of the cut pieces is not important. Tofu can be stored a few days, covered with water, and refrigerated. Change water daily.

TOFU

VINEGAR Cider vinegar is used for pickling and Sweet-and-Sour Sauce (page 142); rice vinegar may be substituted, but do not use red wine vinegar unless specified.

*VINEGAR, CHINESE BLACK Mild but salty. Used for Pickled Pigs' Feet with Ginger (page 167).

WATER CHESTNUTS Fresh water chestnuts have a superior texture and sweeter flavor than canned. Choose ones that feel firm and don't have soft spots.

WHEAT GLUTEN (See DAO POK.)

*WINTER MELON Large melons with a chalky green skin, light spongy texture, and flavor similar

WATER CHESTNUTS

to cucumber; used in soup. Varies in size like pumpkins. Cut sections are some-times available.

WONTON WRAPPERS (or wonton skins) Often available in the produce sec-tion or frozen foods section of supermarkets. Wrappers vary in thickness to appeal to different preferences; a one-pound package usually contains about 50 to 60 wrappers.

*WOOD EARS A dried tree fungus with a smoky flavor and crunchy texture, with more body than cloud ears. Require soaking.

*YELLOW BEAN SAUCE (See BROWN BEAN SAUCE.)

INDEX

conversion chart
EQUIVALENT IMPERIAL AND METRIC MEASUREMENTS

American cooks use standard containers, the 8-ounce cup and a tablespoon that takes exactly 16 level fillings to fill that cup level. Measuring by cup makes it very difficult to give weight equivalents, as a cup of densely packed butter will weigh considerably more than a cup of flour. The easiest way therefore to deal with cup measurements in recipes is to take the amount by volume rather than by weight. Thus the equation reads:

1 cup = 240 ml = 8 fl. oz.   ½ cup = 120 ml = 4 fl. oz.

It is possible to buy a set of American cup measures in major stores around the world.

In the States, butter is often measured in sticks. One stick is the equivalent of 8 tablespoons. One tablespoon of butter is therefore the equivalent to ½ ounce/15 grams.

LIQUID MEASURES

Fluid Ounces	U.S.	Imperial	Milliliters
	1 teaspoon	1 teaspoon	5
¼	2 teaspoons	1 dessertspoon	10
½	1 tablespoon	1 tablespoon	14
1	2 tablespoons	2 tablespoons	28
2	¼ cup	4 tablespoons	56
4	½ cup		110
5		¼ pint or 1 gill	140
6	¾ cup		170
8	1 cup		225
9			250, ¼ liter
10	1¼ cups	½ pint	280
12	1½ cups		340
15		¾ pint	420
16	2 cups		450
18	2¼ cups		500, ½ liter
20	2½ cups	1 pint	560
24	3 cups		675
25		1¼ pints	700
27	3½ cups		750
30	3¾ cups	1½ pints	840
32	4 cups or 1 quart		900
35		1¾ pints	980
36	4½ cups		1000, 1 liter
40	5 cups	2 pints or 1 quart	1120

SOLID MEASURES

U.S. and Imperial Measures		Metric Measures	
Ounces	Pounds	Grams	Kilos
1		28	
2		56	
3½		100	
4	¼	112	
5		140	
6		168	
8	½	225	
9		250	¼
12	¾	340	
16	1	450	
18		500	½
20	1¼	560	
24	1½	675	
27		750	¾
28	1¾	780	
32	2	900	
36	2¼	1000	1
40	2½	1100	
48	3	1350	
54		1500	1½

OVEN TEMPERATURE EQUIVALENTS

Fahrenheit	Celsius	Gas Mark	Description
225	110	¼	Cool
250	130	½	
275	140	1	Very Slow
300	150	2	
325	170	3	Slow
350	180	4	Moderate
375	190	5	
400	200	6	Moderately Hot
425	220	7	Fairly Hot
450	230	8	Hot
475	240	9	Very Hot
500	250	10	Extremely Hot

Any broiling recipes can be used with the grill of the oven, but beware of high-temperature grills.

EQUIVALENTS FOR INGREDIENTS

all-purpose flour—plain flour
coarse salt—kitchen salt
cornstarch—cornflour
eggplant—aubergine

half and half—12% fat milk
heavy cream—double cream
light cream—single cream
lima beans—broad beans

scallion—spring onion
unbleached flour—strong, white flour
zest—rind
zucchini—courgettes or marrow